This book is to be returned on or ⌐
the last date stamped below.

STEP by STEP
TENNIS
SKILLS

Deutscher Tennis Bund

HAMLYN

Photographs:
Front jacket: Michael Cole Camerawork
Back jacket: Fotos BLV Archiv Sport

All photographs by Fotos BLV Archiv Sport except the following:
Colorsport: titlespread; Thomas Exler: pages 5 centre and
bottom, 21, 26, 30, 40, 47, 52, 60, 62, 76, 100, 126, 132,
141; Hans Rauchensteiner: pages 5 top, 6, 8, 23, 70, 85, 88,
129, 134, 137, 142

Artwork: Barbara Von Damnitz
Design: Anton Walter and Robert Mathias

Published by
The Hamlyn Publishing Group Limited
a division of the Octopus Group plc
Michelin House, 81 Fulham Road
London SW3 6RB
and distributed for them by
Octopus Distribution Services Limited
Rushden, Northamptonshire NN10 9RZ, England

English translation copyright © The Hamlyn Publishing Group Limited 1988

Title of the original German edition *Lehrbuch Tennis* by
Deutscher Tennis Bund (German Tennis Federation)
Copyright © 1986 BLV Verlagsgesellschaft mbH, München

English translation first published in 1988

ISBN 0 600 55773 1

Printed in Spain

CONTENTS

Foreword 6
Introduction 7

BASICS

Analysing movements 11
Tactics 15
Common elements for all strokes 16
Breakdown of stroke techniques 25

STROKE TECHNIQUES

Ground strokes 27
Topspin 41
Slicing 53
Lobbing 63
Serving 77
Smashing 88
Volleying 101
Drop shots 111
Half volleying 119
Variations in stroke techniques 124

FOOTWORK

Vital groundwork 127
Starting positions 133
Take-off and running 135
Footwork at the moment of impact 138
Returning to starting positions 143

FOREWORD

The Lawn Tennis Association is pleased to be associated with this extremely well-written and illustrated instructional book by the German Tennis Federation on the techniques of the game.

Step-by-Step Tennis Skills is suitable reading for the beginner through to high level competitor. The wealth of detail illustrated by the excellent sequence photographs should prove invaluable to all players wishing to improve their skills.

It covers the complete range of strokes and techniques which form the basis of sound matchplay. Having studied this excellent book on technique, the reader will find that linked with the relevant strategies it will provide a firm foundation for their development and further enjoyment of their tennis.

Charles Applewhaite
Director of Coaching
Lawn Tennis Association

INTRODUCTION

The main aim of this book is to describe and explain tennis techniques as fully as possible. By techniques we specifically mean the various strokes and such elements as grip and arm and leg movements used to achieve them. Topics such as methodology, training, psychology and tennis injury are not covered.

This book isn't intended to be read through from start to finish, but rather used as a handbook which can be picked up for guidance about individual techniques. You can concentrate on and practise individual strokes and techniques but of course they aren't played in isolation and elements are common to some or all of them, so inevitably there is overlapping and repetition in the descriptions.

For every stroke there is material on the classic version of the shot, acceptable variations and common mistakes. Study the essential points thoroughly and learn to avoid the common mistakes. It is in the area of acceptable variations that you have scope for a personal style. But remember that even world-class players' individual styles, however distinctive, are all based on solid basic techniques.

For the sake of simplicity and clarity all movements relate to right-handed players: left-handers will have to adapt them as appropriate.

Rüdiger Bornemann
Hartmut Gabler
Jock Reetz

BASICS

Before considering techniques and tactics in detail you need to understand the aims of the game at their most basic so you can relate what you do and how you achieve it to these aims.

Basic aims

The essential element of the game of tennis consists in hitting a ball with a racket out of your own court over the net into your opponent or opponents' court.

In the competitive game your goal consists of delivering the ball in such a way that your opponent can't reach the ball which has been played into his or her court or can only return it into the net or out.

You can score with offensive and defensive play by either directly winning points, or forcing your opponent to lose points, or avoiding losing points yourself, in order to win games, sets and matches.

Points can of course be won on the very first shot but in practice several exchanges are normally played before a single point is scored by one or other player.

In non-competitive play you can come to completely different arrangements, for example, to play the ball to each other so that no errors are made, resulting in as long a rally as possible.

Main playing areas

Play from different areas of the court is determined either by the rules (for instance the requirement to serve from the baseline), or by the progress of the game and the direction and force with which the ball is hit. The main areas can be broadly divided into positions
- on the baseline
- in the service line area
- at the net.

Stroke strategies

In making a stroke in tennis you can have different detailed aims, although the overall aim in competition is always to score, whether immediately or not, or whether by gaining a point positively or making your opponent lose one.

Aims for individual shots could be
- to hit the ball in such a way that your opponent can't reach it, for an immediate point
- to hit the ball in such a way that your opponent is put under pressure, for example, by being made to run, or placed in a difficult striking position, to prepare for winning a point of your own or forcing your opponent to lose a point on the following stroke
- to hit the ball in such a way as to avoid losing points yourself
- in the non-competitive game, to hit the ball in such a way that the pre-arranged play is achieved.

Ball flight and bounce behaviour

To make the best of your strokes, you need to understand and be familiar with the way a tennis ball moves and bounces.

The important elements of a tennis ball's behaviour in flight are
- direction (from straight forward to cross court)
- height (from level to high)
- speed (from slow to fast)
- spin (forward, backward, side spin).

Racket movement

To achieve the direction and/or bounce necessary for your particular shot your racket must be moved in a specific way in hitting the ball. In particular the features of this movement can be divided into
- the speed of the head of the racket in hitting the ball, as this substantially determines the speed of the ball struck
- the direction of the hitting movement in relation to where you want the ball to travel (across court, straight forward, level, high)
- the direction of the hitting movement in relation to any spin you want to give the ball
- the position of the racket face on meeting the ball, as this affects both the height of the ball's flight and the spin of the ball.

Player's movement

Try to think of the racket hitting the ball as an extension of your arm. Of course it's not only the movement of your hand, or even arm, which achieves the contact between racket and ball. The whole body can be involved.

No shot is ever exactly the same as another one, although certain types of shot are classed together. Because of this, techniques and ideals for types of shot can't be constant and invariable. However, broadly similar classes of strokes tend to have similar elements which have been identified and basic techniques for each classic type of shot can be adapted to specific circumstances.

Both general movement and specific stroke techniques are affected by a player's individual qualities
● physical build, including height and suppleness
● physical capabilities, for instance co-ordination, strength, stamina, speed
● mental factors such as motivation and intelligence.

Additionally external factors will have an effect.
● the behaviour of the approaching ball
● the features of the court (condition, size)
● the properties of the racket and its stringing
● the weather (wind, sun)
● the actions of the opponent(s) (and partner, where appropriate).

The most important element of sound strokes, however, is good footwork. There are, for example, various appropriate starting positions in the baseline or service line areas which enable you to move off in various directions, and there are different running techniques for moving to the various positions. The basics and specifics of footwork are described in the third section.

Phases of strokes

Stroke techniques can usefully be divided into four phases
● movements made while the ball is approaching, when the racket must be moved so that it encounters the ball in the appropriate way to achieve the trajectory and/or bounce required
● movements made in the lifting phase, preparing for the hitting phase
● movements made during the hitting phase, which should lead to the correct stroke being made
● movements made in the follow-through phase, as this is not only the culmination of the hitting movement, but also reveals how the ball has been struck.

You can see from what has already been covered that there are many different conditions affecting a stroke played in tennis, some of which are under your control and some of which aren't.

Analysing movements

Tennis textbooks have usually started with a sequence analysis in which the three following phases are described one after another, without differentiating their importance: the lifting movement (in the sense of a preparation phase), the hitting movement (with the aim of striking the ball) and the follow-through movement (as a culmination of the hitting movement).

However, using this method of presentation gives no guide to the relative importance of the different elements. How important, for example, is a certain shape of the so-called loop in the lift phase, or rising onto the ball of your foot and shifting your weight in the hitting phase, or a well-defined follow-through in the direction of the stroke in the follow-through phase, for the best possible strike of the ball? The exclusive, even if detailed, description of the chronological sequence of movements supplies no clear answers to this question.

In reality certain elements of the sequence, for example the position of the racket face and the locking of your wrist on striking the ball are important elements, while others, like for example the height of the lifting movement and the position of your left arm, are less so. To bring out the true significance of individual phases you can't simply describe the sequence from

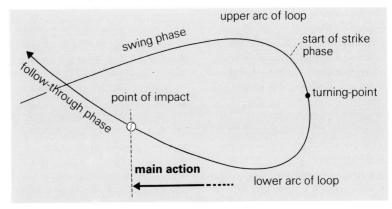

Above: *Scheme of a striking movement with swing, strike and follow-through; the main action is contained within the strike phase.*

Below: *In the main action of the forehand ground stroke the racket is swung forwards and slightly upwards to the point of impact.*

beginning to end, as though all the actions were of equal value. It is far more appropriate and useful to use a method of breaking down the elements of a stroke which highlights the function of the elements. Our system of analysing movements concentrates on the purpose of motion, both the ultimate aim of a sequence of

movements and the contribution towards that of individual elements within the series.

An example should make this clear. On the service the immediate object is merely to hit the ball into your opponent's service court. Breaking this down further, your object can simply consist of bringing the ball into play; in this case your object can be achieved by hitting the ball either from below or from above, without any particular spin. This technique is relatively easy to master, of course, but this kind of serve hardly causes your opponent any difficulties.

If, however, you have the more ambitious goal of putting your opponent under strong pressure through the service by hitting the ball at high speed, then because of specific conditions outside your control (the height and reach of your opponent, the height of the net and the size of the service court, for instance) you will have to hit the ball in such a way that it flies in at least a slightly twisted trajectory. From this it can be established which actions are necessary, or more or less useful, in achieving this.

Movements and techniques are influenced and determined by a players' intentions and aims and by external factors and his opponent's play.

MAIN AND AUXILIARY ACTIONS

There are some actions which are so precisely and invariably determined in their sequence that they can be strictly specified, but there are also actions which allow individual deviations in their execution, so that there can also be perfectly valid alternative actions. In the first case it's appropriate to evaluate actions as categorically right or wrong whereas in the second case judgements such as 'appropriate', 'less appropriate' and 'inappropriate' are more useful.

Knowing the purpose of an action, or its intended outcome, and taking into account a player's individual abilities and the circumstances over which he has no control, the next stage is to know what elements of his action are indispensably necessary to achieve the purpose. For instance:

If you have the goal of hitting a ball from your baseline in such a way as to bounce at high speed within and very close to your opponent's baseline (and consequently to have length), you can accomplish it through the following actions:
● you must swing your racket with high acceleration against the approaching ball which will achieve the high ball speed required
● you must swing the racket level, forwards and upwards against the ball and strike the

ball with the racket face vertical to give the ball a forward spin, so that as a result of the downward curved trajectory which this causes it lands in front of your opponent's baseline and so has the desired length without going out
● your wrist must be braced firmly on impact to ensure that the further two aims of accuracy and safety are achieved.

Main action

The phase within the hitting movement of strong acceleration, a relatively level forward and upward directed swing of the racket and striking the ball with vertical racket face and braced wrist is termed the main action. This main action (in this case within a forehand or backhand ground stroke) is absolutely necessary to achieve your goal.

The main action in tennis is always to be found in the strike phase. The strike phase begins before the turning-point and ends with the point of impact. The main action also ends with the point of impact but where it begins can't be exactly pinpointed. This doesn't matter, however, because the only crucial thing is that the features of the main action occur in such a way that they come together in the most effective way at the point of impact.

Secondary actions

There is also a series of auxiliary actions which are useful and appropriate for supporting this main action, but whose form can't be

In the backswing phase the racket is drawn back in an upper arc so that it can flow smoothly into the lower arc of the hitting movement.

closely prescribed.

A bold swing with a flowing, curved transition to the strike phase assists in accelerating the racket. The form of this transition can't be laid down precisely, however, as the necessary acceleration can also be achieved without any pronounced loop.

The positioning of your leading leg means your body weight can be shifted onto it during the strike phase; in the forehand ground stroke the body is turned in the direction of the stroke to intensify the acceleration of the movement and make the hitting action as effective as possible. How the front leg should be positioned and what the distance between the front and back leg should be, however, is highly variable according to how much stability is required and what actions (in particular running movement) are to follow the shot.

Striking the ball at the side and in front of your hip with a fixed wrist helps impart high

speed to the ball: the ball, on impact with the racket face, meets high resistance and is returned with great force. This is especially so, if, in the forehand ground stroke, the forehand grip is used (the various grips are described in detail later in the book).

There are, however, players who use variants of the forehand grip (tending to the centre grip or else to the extreme forehand grip) without it necessarily being particularly detrimental to the result.

A pronounced continuation of the swing action through the strike phase into the follow-through phase helps in

a precise playing of the ball; but a good player can shorten the long follow-through.

Auxiliary actions for assisting in giving the ball a forward spin are principally:
● shifting your centre of gravity downwards in the swing phase, so that the racket can be more easily swung forwards and upwards in the strike phase
● lowering the head of your racket at the start of the strike phase, so that it can be swung forwards and upwards towards the point of impact against the ball and the ball is given the desired forward spin
● rising onto your toes in the strike phase to assist the upward movement
● using the forehand or backhand grip (for the forehand and backhand ground stroke respectively), so that the racket face can be positioned vertically in front of your hip at the moment of striking the ball.

However, none of these auxiliary actions is absolutely

After striking the ball the racket swings wide in the direction of the hitting movement.

necessary; still less can their execution be precisely prescribed: how low must your body's centre of gravity be shifted, how far should your grip be moved in the forehand shot?

Following on from these remarks, a first answer can be given to the question of what should be judged to be right and wrong in tennis technique: the main action needed to accomplish a given movement task is fixed. A deviation from this fixed pattern of movement is incorrect. In the area of auxiliary actions, however, especially within the swing and follow-through phases, but less so with the strike phase, there is to a certain extent such large scope for movement variations, with their respective advantages and disadvantages, that it is difficult to mark their boundaries. Even so, in this case too, they can be regarded as incorrect if they don't appropriately assist the main action, or even as sometimes happens, they completely or partly impede it.

Individual style

Since the auxiliary actions allow relatively large scope for variation, it is in them that the stamp of the individual's own style can best make itself felt. In particular the timing of the swing and follow-through phases offer the greatest scope for variation. These personal characteristics of movement can be termed movement style, and find expression principally in spacing and timing. Features of individuals' pattern and dynamics of movement are for example breadth and rhythm of movement. This is especially true of the service which is often executed in a very individual manner; particularly in terms of the height and breadth of the swing movement leading up to the main action.

These individual characteristics of movement are related to features of the constitution, strength, speed, temperament and motivation of individual players. For example, smaller players often have more energetic and faster movements, while those of larger players are calmer and more precise. High-spirited players tend to favour energetic actions and relatively large backswing movements, and are inclined to marked changes of grip and a very varied technique. Players whose main aim (in terms of their motivation) is to play a defensive game, prefer in contrast quieter, more economic and more precise movements, and so on.

Tactics

If tennis is a matter of overcoming obstacles imposed by the rules and external conditions of the game, and so being able to pursue certain goals, for example to put your opponent under pressure or to keep the ball in play to avoid faults of your own, these goals or tactical objectives take on a special significance.

Tactical behaviour presupposes observation, thought, judgement and decision-making. In competition you must be able to recognize, for example, that your opponent is acting according to a certain tactical plan and that, among other things, your own plans of action must be modified. However, such observation, thought and decision-making very often needs to be done very rapidly and under conditions of high physical and mental stress, because quick actions and reactions are necessary. There are three main categories of action and reaction in playing tennis which relate partly to the pressure of time and partly to individual players' experience and skill.

Reflexes

Intuitive thought and action is a question of immediately grasping a game event, for the most part under great pressure of time, and coming up with a single action in response.

For example, if you play a volley at the net in such a way that your opponent is caught on the wrong foot, you obviously very quickly perceived the direction in which your opponent was running and hit the ball in precisely the opposite direction; however, because of the lack of time, you could scarcely have mentally played through the situation in all its possibilities. Rather, we are dealing here with a frequently practised and reflex thought and action process.

Most of the individual techniques which can be employed in the course of the game under time pressure: ground strokes, volleys, lobs, smashes, stop volleys, returns, passing shots and so on, can be classified as this form of thought and action. They must be practised in training over and over again, so that in competition they will come naturally and effortlessly.

Considered responses

When you can weigh actions against each other in a planned way, when you can decide between various options, we are dealing with considered thought and action. You can consider different possibilities to assess their effectiveness in the given situation. Before serving, for instance, you can weigh up whether you should hit the ball at high acceleration, but with correspondingly high risk, or whether you should rather give the ball a strong forward and side spin to harass your opponent. These sort of responses relate to individual actions for which an instantaneous response isn't needed.

This sort of decision-making becomes much more a matter of thinking on your feet in the context of a number of shots performed consecutively. In a relatively long rally you need to consider which individual actions can be used to bring the rally to a successful conclusion. The process of considering and deciding, however, in this instance, is greatly restricted by the pressure of time. All combinations of techniques, for instance the combination of a service and volley, or of baseline play ended with a dropshot, involve this sort of response.

Strategic play

Sometimes you will be able to plan for a series of strokes or actions without any great pressure of time. If you work out plans of action or strategies for the entire match, for example, this is thinking and acting strategically. Strategic thinking is directed towards tactical principles such as defensive play, attacking play, safety play, alternation between baseline and net play, but also towards principles such as consistent attack on your opponent's weaknesses, or a slice against topspin players, and so on.

Reflex, considered and strategic thinking and action together form what we understand by the term tactics. As this book concentrates on individual stroke techniques, it deals mainly with the first tactical level, the immediate use and application of the particular stroke in specific situations.

However, before doing this,

we still need to take a look at some of the features of movement and principles of the techniques that apply to all strokes. These cover the moment of impact between ball and racket, the ideal place for this to happen in relation to your body, the significance of grip for the way in which the ball is met, as well as the backswing, hit and follow-through phases.

Common elements for all strokes

POINT OF IMPACT

Angle of impact

Even the slightest variations in the timing of your forward swing (the main action) to adjust to the speed of the oncoming ball will lead to differences in the angle between your racket and the

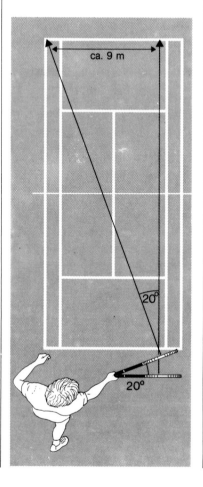

ball at the point of impact and will greatly affect the accuracy of shots in play.

Ideal impact is helped by
● shifting your bodyweight
● turning your upper body for forehand, service, smash and two-handed backhand strokes, or maintaining its position for backhand strokes
● meeting the ball with your wrist and elbow firmly braced.

A firm wrist is particularly important, as even slight movements of your wrist on impact, whether bending, straightening or turning, will result in a wide deviation of the point at which the ball hits your opponent's court.

This is because movements of your wrist obviously produce movements in your racket face and deflect it from the ideal point of impact with the racket face perpendicular to the intended direction of flight at the moment of impact.

A slight forward shift in the point of impact as a result of your wrist being moved only 20 degrees to the left, for example, will lead to an equivalent change in the position of the racket face and so to a deviation of about 9 metres (10 yards) in the point

A 20-degree deviation in angle in the point at which your racket meets the ball produces a change of about 9 m (10 yards) in the point at which the ball crosses your opponent's baseline.

at which the ball crosses the opposite baseline.

Distance from player's body

Ideally, the point of impact between ball and racket for all strokes should be in front of your leading hip. Firstly, this gives a long acceleration path for the racket and good conditions for contact. In

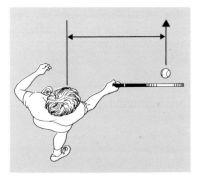

A good lateral distance from the point of impact in the forehand drive ground stroke is achieved by reaching out sideways with a slightly bent arm.

The distance between the shoulder and hitting hand (lever) should be almost the full arm's length, to enable the ball to be played at approximately hip height.

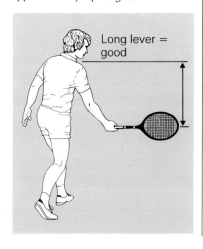

Long lever = good

addition, your centre of gravity is behind the point of impact. The distance to your side from the ball is determined by reaching out with your arm slightly bent and using your arm as a long lever. This also gives a good impact point height, at around hip level, for baseline strokes.

Often, however, the situation of play requires the point of impact to be at a different height
● in the case of a high-bouncing topspin ball, the point of impact is bound to be above shoulder height
● most volleys mean points of impact above hip level
● low bouncing slice shots result in shots being played at knee height or below.

There are disadvantages to hitting the ball from a height
● the shorter lever between the shoulder and the hitting hand has to be compensated for by hitting with greater force; however, the problem changes when responding to a topspin technique, which enables you to accelerate through a lower, more favourable turning point (long lever).
● if the ball is to be played in front of your body, a number of the grips are unsuitable.

There are also problems in hitting a low ball
● to counter the risk of playing the ball out of court, the speed at which you hit the ball should be limited when responding with a straight stroke
● to avoid playing a ball into the net, you may sometimes need to correct the racket face position by rotating your

A high-bouncing ball being played just above shoulder height.

Volleys are often taken between hip and shoulder height.

forearm when responding with a straight stroke. A slice response is better, as the ball rises as a result of the backspin.

- topspin strokes where the point of impact is low are more difficult than those where the point of impact is higher, as they provide only a shallow lower arc with little room for upwards acceleration
- your centre of gravity has to be lowered in good time before the hitting movement.

When serving and playing overhead shots, the location of the point of impact at the height of maximum stretch is determined not only by the need for a long acceleration path but also by the function of the racket as the final element in a sequence of movements that starts from the legs and moves upwards through the body.

The oncoming ball has bounced low, and is met below knee height.

GRIPS

The grip, or the position of the hand on the handle of the racket, has an important part to play in achieving the most effective impact with the ball.

A grip is correct if it enables you to reach a favourable point of impact with the ball in front of your leading hip with the racket face in the appropriate position. It should facilitate the best possible transfer of force.

This section describes some typical grips that you will be able to see being used in competitive tennis. You will see some smooth transitions between two consecutive grips. The recommended grips give the most appropriate position of the racket face at the best point of impact for each stroke, whereas poor and incorrect grips make this position either difficult or impossible.

Forehand grip

In the forehand grip, which is also known as the Eastern grip, with the racket face vertical the hand holds the handle from the right so that the heel of the hand rests against the back (right) broad face of the handle. The back of the hand is directly in line with the flat of the racket.

This grip is recommended for
- strokes on the forehand side

particularly for meeting the ball at hip height and slightly above.

It's wrong or inappropriate for
- backhand strokes
- serving
- smashing

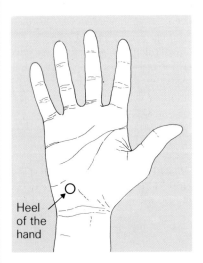

Heel of the hand

The heel of the hand is used as a guide when describing grips.

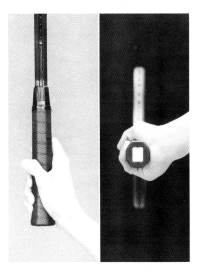

Forehand grip from above and behind (with the racket positioned as at the point of impact). The heel of the hand rests against the right broad plane of the handle.

Extreme forehand grip

In the extreme forehand grip, also known as the Western grip, with the racket face upright the hand holds the handle from the lower right slant position so that the heel rests approximately at the lower right slant of the handle.

This grip is recommended for
● top spin forehand strokes (particularly where the ball is to be hit well above hip height)

It is also a possibility for
● forehand ground shots
● forehand half volleys
● forehand lobs (straight and topspin lobs)

It's wrong and inappropriate for
● forehand slice shots (including slice lobs)
● forehand volleys
● strokes on the backhand side
● serving
● smashing

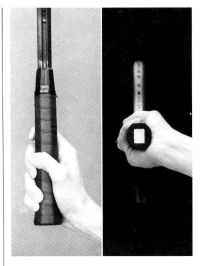

Extreme forehand grip from above and behind (with the racket positioned as at the point of impact). The heel of the hand rests against the lower right slant plane of the handle.

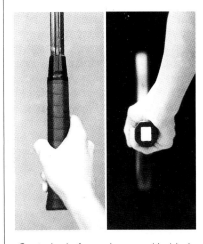

Central grip from above and behind (with the racket positioned as at the point of impact). The heel of the hand rests against the top right slant plane of the handle.

Central grip

In the central grip, also known as the semi-continental grip, with the racket face upright the hand holds the handle from the upper right slant position. The heel then rests

above the upper right slant of the handle.

This grip is possible for
● forehand ground shots (although it isn't possible to play the ball above hip level without making a correction by rotating your lower arm)
● backhand ground shots (with the same correction required as in the forehand)
● forehand volleys
● backhand volleys (in which your wrist has to be stretched and bent)
● serving
● smashing
● lobs
● drop shots

It isn't recommended for
● higher points of impact
If the point of impact is to remain in front of your leading hip, you will need to make an adjustment by rotating your forearm for strokes with a front spin.

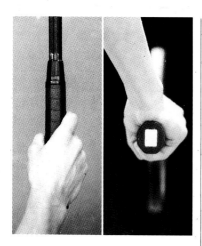

Backhand grip from above and behind (with the racket positioned at the hitting point). The heel of the hand rests on the narrow top plane of the handle.

Two-handed backhand grip from above and behind (with the racket positioned as at the hitting point). The right hand holds the racket in the backhand grip, and the left holds it in the forehand grip.

Backhand grip

In the backhand grip, also known as the continental grip, with the racket face vertical the hand grips the handle from above. The heel of the hand then rests against the top plane of the handle, or alternatively on the top left slant plane in an extreme backhand grip.

This grip is recommended for
- all strokes on the backhand side
- serving
- smashing

It's wrong and inappropriate for
- all forehand strokes

Two-handed backhand grip

The right hand holds the handle from above as in the backhand grip, and rests at the end of the handle. The left hand is positioned immediately in front of the right hand, and holds the handle from the side, as in a left-handed player's forehand grip.

As the left hand is used as well and is also positioned behind the racket handle in relation to the hitting direction, this grip gives a particularly forceful stroke. It also enables a greater acceleration effect to be achieved.

If we assume that the left hand is the hand taking the stroke – with the right hand performing a stabilizing function – it is essential for this hand to be extremely dexterous.

This grip is recommended for
- backhand ground strokes
- backhand topspin strokes

It's also possible for
- backhand slice strokes
- backhand volleys

Summary of grips

	Forehand side	Backhand side
Ground shot	Forehand grip	Backhand grip Two-handed grip
Topspin	Extreme forehand grip	Backhand grip Two-handed grip Extreme backhand grip
Slice	Forehand grip Central grip	Backhand grip Central grip
Volley	Forehand grip Central grip	Backhand grip Central grip
Smash	Backhand grip Central grip	Backhand grip Central grip
Service	Backhand grip Central grip	

THE BACK-SWING PHASE

The backswing prepares for the length and direction of the racket's movement towards the ball. Its potential extent is limited by
● the player's reach
● the mobility of the player's body, shoulders and wrists

Its final form is determined by
● the time available
● the tactical objective and type of stroke
● individual features

Baseline strokes

The upper arc of the loop provides for
● building up the potential energy of the racket's weight
● a smooth transition into the hitting phase.

The time available for the backswing is about 1½ seconds when both players are playing from the baseline, and in extreme cases is only two-fifths of a second for a return. Since the time needed for the total backswing and hitting action in a drive stroke is between six- and nine-tenths of a second, the backswing needs to be shortened only when returning fast services.

The moment for starting the backswing depends on the speed of the oncoming ball and the stroke that you're intending to play. In a slice, for example, you need to swing back earlier, as the total movement is slower than that of a topspin, for instance.

The shape of the loop can differ in its upper arc. A relatively large loop, for example, can assist the racket's acceleration even before the turning point. However, if it's too large it could cause difficulties with early hitting of fast balls. Straight backswing actions make both accelerating your racket and a precise calculation of the point of impact difficult, as the racket speed is initially decelerated before the forward swing, and then has to be re-accelerated.

Even at world class level, analysis shows that different players adopt quite different backswing actions. However, with the different backswing and hitting speeds in other situations, they will remain virtually unchanged for a given player.

Note here the high upper arc loop used in the backswing for a topspin stroke.

This variability of action has clearly developed as a result of players' different backgrounds: the ways in which they have learned to play and in the development of their own personal style. The resulting variations are produced by different ways of starting, and not always the same form of movement of the hand, forearm and upper arm and body.

The length and breadth of the backswing action can be increased or reduced, depending on the situation. This can be achieved by:
● turning the upper part of your body backwards
● reaching outwards (in the forehand) or bringing your forearm closer to your body (in the backhand)
● bending your knees
● opening your wrist (for forehand strokes) or closing it (on backhand stroke), the wrist opening or closing to a greater extent at the end of the fast swing actions as a result of centrifugal force; i.e. the head of the racket is taken further back in each case. Avoid deliberately extreme opening of your wrist in slow strokes.

Volleys and half volleys

As the time available in a volley is often less than six- to nine-tenths of a second, your racket should be taken back only a short distance. It has to be raised above the intended hitting height as the volley is generally given a backspin.

The backswing action for a half volley is similar to that for a ground stroke. However, given the shorter time available, the loop has to be shallower and shorter.

Service and smash strokes

The longer path of acceleration needed for these powerful strokes is established in the backswing phase by
● a long pendulum action with your arm and racket, or in the smash, for reasons of time, lifting your racket above your shoulder
● an ideal curve or loop shape (used even for acceleration)
● opening your wrist, as a result of centrifugal force
● bending and turning your upper body backwards
● bending your knees

An opposite upwards motion of your left arm in the smash is used to counterbalance the force of the movement.

THE STRIKING PHASE

The most effective hitting rhythm requires a smooth transition from the backswing to the hitting phase and a gradual increase in racket acceleration to the point of impact.

Baseline strokes

The hitting phase begins at the start of the racket's acceleration, before the turning point of the loop (see diagram on page 12). To achieve a virtually straight, or only slightly curved, acceleration path you must bring your racket underneath the intended point at which the ball is to be hit (in the case of forward spin) or above it (in the case of backspin) as early as possible.

You must co-ordinate all the component parts of the action so you don't waste movement and energy in the overall movement and, in particular, so you achieve the best stroke possible. This involves using your muscles in sequence from the bottom upwards, and from the inside outwards.

The exact timing and dynamics of the different elements of the action in relation to one another is vital where you need a high hitting speed as well as accuracy. In this case the hitting action must begin from your legs, and continue through your body, your arm and your hand. Your wrist must be fixed in

position early: this applies particularly in a bending and stretching direction. Your hitting action needs to be planned in good time in terms of space, time and dynamics, as there is little possibility of making adjustments to it in the forward swing phase.

Volleys

Volleys normally entail the ball moving at very high speed and so rebounding with considerable force. In these cases it's useful to hit the ball with backspin. The main reasons for this are
● that the required flight of the ball is achieved even with low racket speeds
● the ball bounces low, to the player's advantage.

The volley hit with a backspin also has the advantage that you can execute it in a more leisurely and so more controlled manner, which is particularly useful where the point at which you hit the ball is low. In addition, co-ordination between your armswing and forward and downward body movement is better as the direction and acceleration of the two movements can be properly harmonized.

When the ball is hit in a rising trajectory, the chances of hitting are better, as the downwards hitting action to some extent goes into the trajectory of the oncoming ball.

In the service, the legs are already at full stretch when the racket is still at the lowest point of the loop.

The inwardly rotating movement of the arm continues after the ball has been hit.

Free hitting side: the shoulder line points very steeply upwards, with the right shoulder positioned vertically above the left foot.

Service and smash strokes

In the service and smash the hitting action needs to achieve an extremely high ball speed as well as reliability and reasonable accuracy. This involves excellent co-ordination between the different elements of the movement.

You need to begin the hitting phase by rising onto the balls of your feet, straightening your ankles and knees. This must be followed immediately by contracting the muscles in your lumbar region, your abdomen, chest, shoulder, arm and hand (the hitting muscles). Co-ordinating a whiplike action means that your ankles and knees must be straightened right from the moment when the wrist is still opening in

preparation on the arm loop action and your elbow is bending increasingly. The loop is then at the optimum lowest point, when your hitting muscles are pre-extended to a little less than their maximum; your hitting hand is then behind your head, just above the level of the nape of your neck. To achieve a stroke perpendicular to the direction of the ball's flight your forearm needs to be rotated just before the point of impact. This action is visibly continued in the follow-through.

During the course of the hitting action you must bring your right shoulder into a position almost vertically above your left foot, the line of your shoulders pointing steeply upward. Only with this free

hitting side is it possible for all the groups of muscles involved to be used to the full for accelerating your racket. It also enables you to gain the maximum height of impact possible.

Your left arm, which has been stretched upwards as the ball is raised, is lowered at the start of the hitting action, and is then bent across your body as the action continues. This counter-action improves your hitting accuracy and reliability.

THE FOLLOW-THROUGH PHASE

This is the completion of the stroke after the ball has been hit. The movement and force of the stroke can't be abruptly halted immediately after impact, but continues with reducing speed and force.

Breakdown of stroke techniques

Having looked at the basics, we can now describe and analyse individual stroke techniques. We shall do this in four stages, each stage being broken down in turn into a number of part-stages.

Basic factors
We begin by considering the situations in which the technique is used: as a ground stroke from the baseline area, say. This stage also covers such physical features as the dimensions of the court, the height of the net and also dimensions such as the player's reach.

We then ask what are the tactical uses to which the technique can be sensibly put in this situation.

Then, on the basis of physical laws, we consider the intended flight of the ball (with a slight forward rotation at relatively high speed in the case of this stroke) to achieve the goal, or objective.

Main and secondary actions
Now we can consider the conditions that relate to a player's actions: we have to see what you need to do for the ball to travel as you intend, in line with your objectives.

Here, we begin by looking at the main points of meeting the ball, as it is the way in which the ball is met that will determine its subsequent flight.

We then look at the secondary actions that support the hitting or main action, in the backswing, hitting and follow-through phases.

Acceptable variations
In the next stage, we deal with permissible deviations from the classic technique, with their advantages and disadvantages. These relate to the secondary actions in the swing, hitting and follow-through phases.

Common mistakes
Finally, we cover some errors commonly made in the main and secondary actions.

Ground strokes

In which situations and positions are these strokes used, and with what tactical objectives?

What effects do they have on the ball's behaviour?

Court positions
Ground strokes, both forehand and backhand, are generally played from the baseline area.

Tactical uses
● To play the ball reliably over the net.
● Where possible, to hit the ball far enough for it to bounce between the service line and the baseline, forcing your opponent to remain at the baseline. This creates a baseline rally.
● In baseline rallies preferably to hit the ball cross court, as the net is lower in the middle than at the sides (reliability), the trajectory is longer than in the case of a stroke down the line (reliability, possibility of more power input and momentum), you can deviate sideways without the ball going out of court, and you have a shorter distance to travel to return to the most advantageous position after playing the stroke.
● To put your opponent under pressure, with a well-placed and, where possible, relatively fast ball.
● Possibly to use the ground stroke as a forerunner to a net attack where a ball is played shorter by your opponent, by

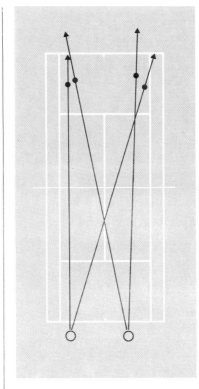

Forehand and backhand ground strokes can be played parallel to the sidelines or across the court. Where possible, they should bounce between the service line and the baseline.

The ball flies over the net at a height of up to 2 m (6 ft) at average speed and with a slight forward spin.

playing as deep as possible towards your opponent's baseline.
● To get past your opponent when he makes a net attack.
● The passing shot should primarily be played parallel to the sidelines when your opponent is positioned close to the net, and his attacking ball was very long.
● The passing shot should, where possible, be played across when your opponent is still on the service line, when he is running forwards, or when his attacking ball was relatively short.

Effects on the ball's behaviour
● As the ball is given little spin, its trajectory has to be controlled by the height and speed of its flight.
● For a long and reliable ground stroke, as a rule, you should play the ball about 2 metres (6 feet) above the net, at average speed.
● If the situation allows higher speeds, you should play the ball lower above the net, to prevent it from going out of court.
● The higher the ball's flight curve, the higher it will bounce.

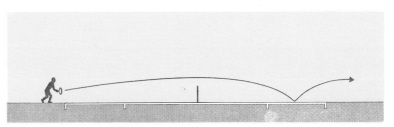

Backswing *The upper body pivots, the weight is shifted onto the right leg, the racket is taken back in the upper arc, and the left leg brought forward into the direction of hitting.*

Striking the ball *The racket head is lowered, the racket swung forwards and slightly upwards, the weight is shifted onto the left leg and the upper body turned.*

| 1 | 2 | 3 | 4 | 5 | 6 |

FOREHAND DRIVE

Basic techniques

This section shows you what you have to do to make the ball do as you intend.

Meeting the ball

• You should swing your racket slightly forwards and upwards, as in photographs 7 and 8, to give the ball some forward spin.
• You should accelerate your racket, particularly its head, to reach the required ball speed.
• You should make a long swing with your racket in the direction of the stroke, as in photographs 6 and 8, to achieve greater accuracy and reliability.
• You should hit the ball to your side in front of your hip, with your wrist braced and your racket face vertical, as in photograph 8, to hit the ball with maximum force.

The backswing phase

• At the beginning of the backswing phase you should hold your racket in the forehand grip so that the racket face can be brought into the upright position to meet the ball.
• Your upper body and right foot should be turned to the right, as in photograph 2: you should take your racket back in the upper arc in such a way as to allow a smooth transition into the hitting phase, as in photographs 3 and 4.
• Your body's centre of gravity should be lowered by bending your knees, as in photograph 3.
• Bring your left leg, which takes most of your weight during the hitting and backswing movements, forward into the intended direction of hitting as in photograph 4; your feet should be approximately hip width apart, to improve your balance.

Meeting the ball *in front of the hip with the wrist firm.*

Follow-through *The racket continues forwards and upwards in the direction of hitting, with the legs straightening.*

7   8   9   10   11   12

The hitting phase

• Your racket should be lowered in the transition to the hitting phase (photographs 5 and 6), so that it can be swung forwards and upwards.
• Your body weight should be shifted to your front leg as in photographs 5 and 7, and your body should be turned in the direction of hitting as the hitting action is delivered (see photographs 7 and 8). This helps accelerate the racket and ensure the best stroke possible.
• To assist the upwards movement, you should begin to straighten your legs.
• Your right arm remains reaching out sideways.

The follow-through phase

• You should continue to swing your racket in the same direction after hitting the ball (see photographs 9 to 12). If you don't do this, your acceleration into the stroke and control on impact will be impaired.
• Your legs should continue to be straightened.

FOREHAND DRIVE

Acceptable variations

The backswing phase

- Many players play the forehand drive ground stroke with the centre grip: they may well find it easier, but it has the disadvantage of lessening the power behind the stroke and the ball can't be met sufficiently far in front of the body.
- Topspin players also often use the extreme forehand grip for the forehand drive ground stroke.
- Many players play the stroke with a backswing in which the upper arc of the loop is shallow. Although this can have the advantage of saving time and increasing the accuracy of movement, it can have the disadvantage of hampering the flow of the movement and so reducing acceleration.
- The upper arc of the loop itself can be executed in a number of different ways.
- The sideways-on position varies according to circumstances: it is more open the more the ball is to be hit

The backswing, with a high upper arc and open position: this also makes it possible to hit the ball without giving it any spin.

across the court, the more the stroke is intended as a preparation for a net attack, and the more a player prefers the Western grip. It does, however, entail a risk in that it reduces your control over the ball.
- The timing/dynamics may take an individual form, particularly on the transition between the racket being taken back in the backswing phase and accelerated in the strike phase.

The striking phase

- The time at which the racket is brought down to below the subsequent point of impact with the ball varies. The earlier this happens, the greater the accuracy and control with which your racket

Open position in the backswing to a forehand drive ground stroke.

can be swung to the point of impact.
- The upper body can be pivoted to a greater or lesser degree. This assists in accelerating your racket.
- The initial speed and acceleration of the racket in hitting can vary. More continuous acceleration of your racket to the point of impact results in a more reliable and controlled impact with the ball.
- The more explosive the action of rising onto the balls of your feet, the more likely it is that you will find yourself with both feet off the ground on meeting the ball.

The follow-through

- The greater the speed of the strike and the more emphatic the shift of the body weight, the longer the follow-through continues.

Common mistakes

The backswing phase

● Using the backhand grip
This prevents you from achieving the upright positioning of the racket face when meeting the ball at the point of impact.
● No, or little, turning of the upper body
This prevents you from taking the racket back sufficiently far, resulting in a punching action at the point of impact.
● Swinging back extremely late
This reduces your chances of meeting the ball at the right time, and leads to an uncontrolled stroke.
● Swinging very short or long
With an excessively short swing you can't accelerate the racket sufficiently, and if your swing is too long you risk meeting the ball too late, and so reducing the accuracy of your stroke.
● Swinging very wide or narrow
The smoothness of the movement is often lost as a result of a swing which is too wide or narrow: you can't meet the ball early enough, particularly in a wide swing; generally the force of the stroke is reduced.

The striking phase

● Lack of smooth transition
An obvious pause between the backswing and hitting movements affects the uniform acceleration of your stroke.
● Failing to lower the head of

Leaning backwards on delivering the stroke adversely affects the way the ball is met and prevents you from shifting your weight forwards.

the racket
If you don't bring your racket below the subsequent point of impact you won't be able to swing it forwards and upwards.
● Reaching upwards too early
This interferes mainly with the forwards and upwards swing.
● Leaning backwards
This means that your weight

The point of meeting the ball is too far away from the body. This lessens the power of the swing and stroke acceleration.

isn't transferred from your back leg to your front leg, leading to a reduction in the acceleration of the movement and so impairing the meeting with the ball.
● No swing action
This often leads to a punching type of stroke in the hitting phase.
● Too early inward turning of the hip and upper body
Poor co-ordination between the armswing and inward rotation of your body into the direction of the stroke leads to a jerky, uncontrolled stroke action.
● Being too late in meeting the ball.
● Meeting the ball too near or too far from your body
Both these faults lead to a reduction in the acceleration of the movement and adversely affect the way in which the ball is met.
● Wrist not firm on meeting the ball
This greatly impairs your control on meeting the ball.

The follow-through phase

● Finishing too early
Ending the follow-through movement as a result of a blockage in the flow of your movement or bending your wrist or elbow too early interferes badly with ball control.

Follow-through *The racket continues forwards and upwards, in the direction of the stroke, with the legs straightening.*

Striking the ball *The racket head is lowered, the racket swung forwards and upwards, with an early shift of the weight onto the front leg, the*

| 12 | 11 | 10 | 9 | 8 | 7 |

BACKHAND DRIVE

Basic techniques

This section shows you what you have to do to make the ball do as you intend.

Meeting the ball

● You should swing your racket slightly forwards and upwards to give the ball some forward spin.
● You should accelerate your racket, particularly the racket head, to achieve the required ball speed.
● You should make a long swing with your racket in the direction of the stroke (as in photographs 7 to 9) to achieve greater accuracy and reliability.
● You should hit the ball to your side, in front of your hip (even further forward than in the forehand drive), with your wrist firm and your racket face upright (photograph 9) to hit the ball with maximum force.

The backswing phase

● At the start of the backswing phase, you should hold your racket in the backhand grip so that the racket face can be brought into an upright position to meet the ball.
● The backswing movement is started by your left hand taking the racket back by the neck of the racket, as in photograph 3, to stabilize the backswing and allow your upper body to be turned further to the left.
● Your upper body is turned well back and you take up a sideways-on stance with your right foot forward so that the back of your right shoulder is pointing towards the net as in photograph 5: this assists the accelerating armswing in the direction of the stroke.
● Take your racket in the upper arc of the loop; the loop should be smaller than for the forehand drive ground stroke.

upper body is firm, the ball is met to the side and in front of the hip, and the wrist is firmly braced.

Backswing *The upper body is turned sharply, the racket is taken back in the upper arc, supported by the left hand, and a sideways-on position adopted.*

| 6 | 5 | 4 | 3 | 2 | 1 |

The striking phase

• Your centre of gravity should be lowered by bending your knees.
• You should lower the head of your racket in the transition to the hitting phase, as in photographs 6 and 7, so you can swing forwards and upwards in the main action.
• Your feet should be at least your hips' width apart, as in photograph 8, to improve your balance.
• Your body weight should be shifted onto your front leg at the start of the hitting phase, to assist in acclerating your racket. The shift of weight takes place earlier than in the forehand drive and your upper body is turned only until the point of your shoulder points in the direction of the stroke, as in photographs 8 and 9.
• You maintain the sideways-on position of your feet and body as shown in photographs 6 to 9.

• Shortly before meeting the ball you extend your right arm, as in photographs 7 and 8, to hit the ball with the maximum force.

The follow-through phase

You continue swinging your racket in the direction of the stroke, as in photographs 10 to 12. At the end of the follow-through phase, your racket and the right side of your body point in the direction of the stroke, as in photograph 12.

33

BACKHAND DRIVE

Acceptable variations

The backswing phase
- Many players play backhand strokes with the central grip: this may well seem easier, but it has the disadvantage that the transfer of force is less than ideal, and you can't meet the ball sufficiently far in front of your body.
- Many players don't take the racket into the upper arc of the loop until late in the backswing phase; although this can have the advantage of improving the smoothness of movement, it can prevent you from getting to the lower arc of the loop at the right time. There are various alternative versions of the loop itself.
- The timing/dynamics may vary between individuals, particularly in the transition between the backward swing of the racket in the preparatory phase and its acceleration in the strike phase.

The striking phase
- Deviations in the hitting phase of the backhand drive are very restricted and are hardly worth mentioning.

The follow-through phase
- The higher the speed of stroke, the longer the follow-through will be.
- With a high-speed stroke and maintaining the sideways-on hitting position, the racket follows a steep upward swing.

High follow-through in the backhand drive ground stroke, still maintaining the sideways-on position.

Common mistakes

The backswing phase
- Using the forehand grip
This means that the face of the racket can only be brought upright to meet the ball at the desired point of impact by bending your wrist.
- Little or no turning of the upper body and extremely short backswing
These prevent you from adequately accelerating your racket to strike the ball, often resulting in a punching action.
- Swinging back extremely late
This reduces your chance of meeting the ball at the right time, and leads to an uncontrolled stroke.
- Swinging extremely wide
This reduces the force of your stroke as the use of your body behind it is limited.

- Failing to support the backswing with the left hand
This often means that your body is not turned far enough backwards and your control of the movement, particularly on the transition between the backswing and striking phase, is lessened.

The striking phase
- Failing to take up a sideways-on position
This hinders you from swinging your arm in the desired direction of hitting.
- Not lowering the head of the racket
Failing to bring your racket below the subsequent point of impact prevents you from swinging your racket forwards and upwards.
- Straightening the legs too early
This adversely affects your forward and upward swing, in particular.
- Leaning backwards

Straightening the legs too early inhibits the forwards and upwards swing of the racket.

Moving out of the sideways-on striking position too early leads to a lack of accuracy in meeting the ball, and a lack of accuracy in targeting.

If the ball is met very late the racket will have too little momentum and the force of the stroke and control of the ball will be impaired.

This means that there is no shift of weight onto your front leg, which reduces the acceleration of your racket and leads to an uncontrolled meeting of the ball.
● No swing movement
This often leads to the ball being hit with a punching stroke in the hitting phase.
● Abandoning the sideways-on position too early
If your entire body turns in the action of hitting the ball, it will seriously impair your control of the ball.
● Meeting the ball too late or too far from the body
Both these mistakes lead to a reduction in the acceleration of your movement, and so to decreased control.
● Wrist not firm on meeting the ball
This has a serious effect on your control of the ball.
● Failing to straighten arm just before meeting the ball
This indicates a deceleration of momentum in your hitting

action, with the point of impact too close to the side of your body.

The follow-through phase
● Ending the follow-through movement far too early by stopping the flow of movement.
● Deviating from the direction of the stroke too early
This mistake and the one

If the wrist is excessively bent in the follow-through, it indicates that the momentum of the hitting action was decelerated very early and the power behind the stroke was limited.

above demonstrate that your control of the ball wasn't sound.
● Marked, increasing bending of the wrist
This indicates that the momentum has been stopped very early, your wrist was not firm, and the transfer of force to the ball was limited.

Follow-through *The racket continues forwards and upwards in the direction in which the ball has been hit.*

Striking the ball *The racket swings forwards and upwards, and at the same time the weight is shifted onto the right foot, turning the*

upper body. The point at which the ball is met is in front of the hip, with the wrists firm and the arms almost fully extended.

| 12 | 11 | 10 | 9 | 8 | 7 |

TWO-HANDED BACKHAND

Basic techniques

This section shows you what you have to do to make the ball do as you intend.

Individual elements of style are illustrated in the grip, the backswing (photograph 2), the early use of the body in the strike phase (photographs 8 and 9) and hitting with the left arm bent (photographs 8 and 10).

Meeting the ball

- You should swing your racket slightly forwards and upwards to impart a slight forward spin to the ball.
- You should accelerate your racket head so that it reaches its highest speed at the point of meeting the ball.
- You should swing your racket as far as possible in the direction in which the ball is hit, as in photographs 8 to 11, to achieve greater accuracy and reliability.
- You should play the ball in front of your right hip with the face of your racket upright, and your wrists braced, as in photograph 10, to increase your control over the ball and so that you hit it with full force.

Backswing *The upper body is turned well back, the racket carried back, a definite sideways-on* *position taken up and the body's centre of gravity shifted downwards.*

6 5 4 3 2 1

The backswing phase

● At the beginning of the backswing phase you should hold your racket with your right hand in the backhand grip and in your left hand with the forehand grip.
● Your upper body is turned well towards the back (with your right hip pointing towards the net) to give adequate room for the backswing, as shown in photographs 2 and 3.
● During the backswing movement, your right leg moves forwards and across towards the ball.
● As a result of the two-handed racket grip, your racket has to be taken back in a rather flattened upper arc, as shown in photographs 1 to 5.

The striking phase

● Your centre of gravity is lowered by bending your knees so that your body can be brought not just forwards, but also upwards at the same time.
● At the start of the hitting action, plant your right foot in the direction of the oncoming ball, at least a shoulder's width in front of your foot. Your body weight is transferred onto your right leg during the hitting phase, as in photograph 6.
● As a result of both your hands firmly holding the handle your upper body has to turn in the direction in which the ball is to be hit, as in photographs 8 to 10, which gives a supporting effect for acceleration.
● At the start of the striking phase your left arm is extended so that both arms are normally fully extended in the main action.

The follow-through phase

● You continue swinging your racket in the direction in which the ball has been hit, as shown in photographs 11 and 12.

37

TWO-HANDED BACKHAND

Acceptable variations

There are few possibilities for varying the two-handed backhand as both hands are firmly holding the racket.

The backswing phase
● Many players hold the racket with both hands in the forehand grip and take the backswing with their elbows bent, so that the movement sweeps close to their body.

The striking phase
● Players who play a two-handed backhand have a tendency to shift their body weight forward less when they hit the ball hard, and as a result often end up leaning backwards. This is because they can't counterbalance the movement with their left arm; the same can also happen in difficult situations caused mainly by fast body movements.
● Particularly in fast hitting movements, the body's centre of gravity can be shifted in the direction of hitting, beyond the right leg, which means your balance needs to be restored by bringing forward the left leg.
● The left arm can be slightly bent until the point of impact.

The follow-through phase
● Many players occasionally let go of the racket handle with their left hand after playing the ball, and follow through with their right hand only.

If both arms are bent too much when the ball is hit, the momentum of the shot suffers.

● In a particularly powerful stroke the follow-through may be continued as far as the right shoulder.

Common mistakes

The backswing phase
● Turning the upper body too little
This results in an over-short backswing which provides too

little impetus, with the ball being hit in a punching-type stroke.
● Legs too close together
This prevents your body weight from being transferred forward correctly in the hitting phase.
● Failing to bring the right arm back close to the body, and far enough back
This restricts your possible momentum in the hitting phase.

The striking phase
● Straightening the legs too early
This results in a loss of propulsion behind your forward and upward stroke action.
● Meeting the ball very late
This spoils the reliability and precision of the shot.
● Unfirm wrists
This also impairs the reliability and precision of the stroke.
● Bending both arms too much in the main action
This limits the momentum of your movement into the point of impact.
● Turning the upper body too early
This often means meeting the ball too late and your racket being taken to the right too early, which impairs the reliability, precision and speed of your shot.

The follow-through phase
● Ending the follow-through too early
This severely affects the accuracy with which the ball is played.

Turning the upper body too soon leads to uncontrolled hitting, and often to the ball being played too late.

Topspin

In which situations and positions is this technique used, and what are its uses and results?
What effects does it have on the ball's behaviour?

Court positions
Topspin forehand and backhand drives are played mainly from the baseline area, but also from the centre line area.

Tactical uses
● To make the ball bounce at least as far as the service line, but if possible between the service line and the baseline, forcing your opponent to return the ball to your baseline area (1). This is to ensure that the ball is kept in play.
● A long and well-placed topspin shot puts particular pressure on your opponent. Given the ball's relatively high, fast bounce, he is forced well behind the baseline, or out of court.
● Particularly from the centre of the court, you can play the ball in such a way that it flies across at an extreme angle, and forces your opponent out of his court (2), laying the court open for a follow-up winning shot.
● In response to a ball played shorter by your opponent you can use the topspin forehand primarily as a preparatory shot for a net attack.
● If your opponent is attacking at the net, this technique can also be used as a passing

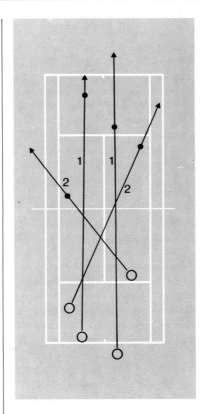

The topspin forehand and backhand are played from both the baseline and the centre of the court, and are designed to keep an opponent at bay.

shot: this applies not only to the conventional shot parallel to the sideline, but also, and more particularly, to the passing shot across the court. However, topspin balls played directly at your opponent and low are also difficult for your opponent to play back as a

volley or half volley, since they have to be met below net height.

Effects on the ball's behaviour
● The ball should fly with a marked forward spin, and should therefore follow a very curved flight path.
● Where a topspin stroke is played long, the ball has to fly over the net at a higher level.
● Balls hit with topspin bounce up from the ground relatively fast and high.

A topspin ball played from the baseline area (1) should bounce between the service line and the baseline.
A topspin ball played from the centre of the court (2) can be played short and across court. The ball travels along a sharply curved flight path, and bounces relatively fast and high.

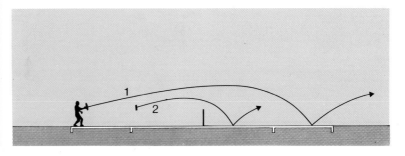

Backswing *The right leg is turned sideways and bent, the upper body is turned and the racket taken back in the upper arc.*

Striking the ball *The head of the racket is taken low, the racket swung steeply forwards and upwards, the bracing leg extended*

| 1 | 2 | 3 | 4 | 5 | 6 |

TOPSPIN FOREHAND

Basic techniques

This section shows you what you have to do to make the ball do as you intend.

Meeting the ball

- You should swing your racket, particularly the head of the racket, sharply forwards and upwards towards the ball, as in photographs 5 to 7, to achieve the required topspin.
- Your racket movement must be very fast, to give the ball the pronounced topspin you want.
- The ball should be played to the side and in front of your leading hip, with the face of your racket upright and your wrist firm, as in photograph 7, to give the most powerful stroke possible.

The backswing phase

- At the beginning of the backswing phase, in the starting position, you should hold your racket in the forehand grip (or possibly the extreme forehand grip) so that the face of the racket can be brought into an upright position to meet the ball and to achieve a forceful stroke.
- Your full weight is transferred onto your right leg, which is used as the push-off or bracing leg in the hitting action, by a turning step to the side, as in photographs 1 to 3.
- You turn your upper body towards the back, take your racket back in the upper arc of the loop, as in photographs 1 and 2, which allows a smooth transition into the hitting phase.
- Lower your centre of gravity by a definite bending of your knees and putting your weight onto your right leg, as in photograph 3.

sharply and the upper body turned. The ball is met to the side and in front of the hip, with the wrist firm.

Follow-through *The racket continues forwards and upwards, then to the left side of the body, with the weight transferred onto the left leg.*

| 7 | 8 | 9 | 10 | 11 | 12 |

The striking phase

● Take the head of your racket very low in the transition to the hitting phase (as shown in photographs 4 and 5) to allow the tip of the racket, particularly, to be swung sharply upwards.
● You begin the snap straightening of your left leg in the smooth transition between the backswing and hitting phase from the more or less open hitting position and the right leg, i.e. the leg nearest the hitting arm, pushes off forcefully from the ground, as in 5 to 7.
● Turn your upper body forwards into the face-on position at the same time as you hit the ball, as in photographs 4 to 7, so that you can swing the racket not only sharply upwards but also forwards, to achieve a powerful stroke.

The follow-through phase

● You continue the sharp forwards and upwards movement of the head of your racket, as in photographs 8 to 10; firstly, this finishes off the stroke, and secondly it shows that the ball has been given the desired spin.
● Finally, you swing your racket to the left side of your body, transferring your weight onto your left leg. The two actions, the arm movement and the transfer of weight, are produced by the movements in the hitting phase, by pushing off from your back leg, and at the same time turning the upper part of your body.

TOPSPIN FOREHAND

Acceptable variations

The backswing phase

- The form of grip can vary; typical topspin players tend, however, to prefer the extreme forehand grip.
- There is a whole series of individual variations for the loop. The backswing movement is often begun by taking the elbow sharply backwards and upwards.
- The position, too, often varies. It tends to be more open the more an extreme forehand grip is used, the greater the use of the body, the more the ball is to be hit across the court, and the more the shot is intended as a preparation for a net attack. It may, however, be played more to the side when the ball is to be played parallel to the sidelines.
- The timing/dynamics can also vary between individual players, particularly in the transition between taking the racket back into the backswing phase, and accelerating it in the hitting phase.

The striking phase

- Many players straighten their push-off leg with such a snap that they find themselves with both feet off the ground just after meeting the ball, or in some cases even just before.
- The hitting action can be assisted by more or less dynamic turning of the upper body.
- With increasingly powerful use of the forearm to increase the speed of hitting the ball, the arm may be bent to a greater or lesser extent in the course of the hitting action.
- When hitting the ball with a straight arm, the fast, sharp upwards movement of the head of the racket is achieved mainly by turning the arm.

The follow-through phase

- Where the forearm is fully extended in the hitting phase,

The backswing movement for a topspin forehand begins with the raising of your elbow.

As a rule, a very open hitting position is adopted in the topspin forehand drive.

For a topspin drive parallel to the sidelines you can hit the ball from a sideways-on position.

the racket is tilted early and tightly towards the left in a windscreen wiper-type action.
• The racket may be swung through over the hitting shoulder. This topspin is generally played with a low point of impact.

Right: The sharp upwards acceleration of the head of the racket is achieved by turning your outstretched hitting arm.

The hitting action is carried out with your arm bent, to exert more power.

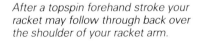

After a topspin forehand stroke your racket may follow through back over the shoulder of your racket arm.

TOPSPIN FOREHAND

Common mistakes

The backswing phase

• Using the centre or backhand grip
This makes it impossible to hit the ball with full force.
• Little or no turning of the upper body
This greatly limits your space in the backswing movement.
• Little bending of the knees
This inhibits the acceleration of your movement.
• Excessively sideways-on position
This makes it difficult to transfer your weight onto and bend your right leg, and hampers the turn of your upper body in the hitting phase.

The striking phase

• Failing to lower the racket head sufficiently
If you don't take your racket below the subsequent point of impact, you won't be able to swing your racket steeply forwards and upwards.
• Straightening the legs too early
This affects the co-ordination of your movement as a whole.
• Leaning backwards
This causes your racket to be swung too steeply upwards so that the forward movement of the racket is largely omitted and the ball doesn't travel far enough into your opponent's court.
• Little racket acceleration
Particularly at the tip of the racket this prevents you from giving the ball sufficient topspin.

Failing to turn the upper body sufficiently limits the breadth of the backswing action.

• Hitting the ball with a straight arm, using only a shoulder movement
This prevents the best possible acceleration of the racket.
• Meeting the ball too far from or too close to the body
This reduces the use of your body behind the stroke.
• Wrist not firm on meeting the ball
This greatly affects your control on meeting the ball.

Hitting with a straight arm using only a shoulder movement prevents the head of the racket from being accelerated as much as it could be.

An excessive sideways-on position often limits the turning of the upper body in the hitting phase.

The follow-through phase

• Extremely short follow-through movement
This indicates deceleration or even total absence of momentum just before the point of impact.

Backswing *The upper body is turned well back and the racket is taken back, supported by the left* *hand. A marked sideways-on position is adopted, with the knees well bent.* **Striking the ball** *With the racket head lowered, the racket is swung steeply forwards and upwards. With the legs straight and standing in a*

1 2 3 4 5 6

TOPSPIN BACKHAND

Basic techniques

This section shows you what you have to do to make the ball do as you intend.

Meeting the ball

- You should swing your racket, particularly the head of the racket, sharply forwards and upwards towards the ball to achieve the required topspin, as shown in photographs 7 to 9.
- The racket movement must be very fast, to give the ball the desired pronounced topspin.
- You play the ball to the side and further in front of your body than in the topspin forehand drive with the face of the racket upright and your wrist firm (as in photograph 9) to enable you to hit the ball with maximum force.

The backswing phase

- The backswing movement is started by taking the racket back with your left hand by the neck of the racket (as shown in photographs 1 and 2), to stabilize the movement and allow your shoulders to be turned further backwards.
- At the start of the backswing phase, you should hold your racket in the backhand grip so that the face of the racket can be brought into an upright position to meet the ball and to achieve an ideal transfer of force.
- Turn your upper body well towards the back; take up a marked sideways-on position so that the back of your right shoulder is pointing towards the net (as in photograph 4); this assists the accelerating armswing in the direction of hitting. To improve your

sideways-on position, the ball is taken to the side and in front of the body with the wrist firm.

Follow-through *The racket continues forwards and upwards in the direction in which the ball has been hit.*

| 7 | 8 | 9 | 10 | 11 | 12 |

balance your feet should be more than your hips' width apart.
● Take your racket back in the upper arc of the loop, as in photographs 2 to 4, to allow a smooth transition into the hitting phase.
● Lower your centre of gravity by an emphatic bending of your knees, and putting your weight onto your right leg.

The striking phase

● Lower your racket, as in photographs 5 to 7, to allow the head of the racket to be swung steeply upwards in the hitting phase (photographs 8 and 9).
● Straighten your legs, particularly the front push-off leg, to assist the sharp upwards movement (photographs 5 and 6).
● Continue to transfer your body weight onto your leading leg, and turn your upper body only until your shoulder line points in the direction of the shot.
● You play the ball with your arm extended, as in photograph 9, reaching out just before the point of impact.

The follow-through phase

● Continue the sharp and upward movement of the racket initially in the direction of the shot, maintaining your sideways-on position. This both rounds off the stroke and demonstrates that you have imparted the appropriate spin to the ball.
● At the end of the follow-through phase, your body turns forwards as a result of the powerful, fast hitting action, resulting in a slightly open position.

TOPSPIN BACKHAND

Acceptable variations

The backswing phase
- The form of backhand grip may vary from one individual to another. Many typical topspin players tend to adopt an extreme backhand grip.
- There is a series of individual variations for the loop.
- The timing/dynamic sequence may vary between individuals, particularly in the transition between taking back the racket in the backswing phase and its acceleration in the hitting phase.

The striking phase
- Many players straighten their push-off leg with such a snap that they find themselves with both feet off the ground just after meeting the ball, or in some cases even just before.
- With extreme exertion of the forearm in the hitting phase and the extreme backhand grip, the arm may be bent to a greater or lesser extent to increase the hitting speed and to intensify the steep upwards movement. This variation does, however, put great demands on the forearm.

The follow-through phase
- Where the body is used to the utmost in the main action it can lead to an open position and a follow-through movement in which the racket ends up pointing in the opposite direction from the

Follow-through from a topspin backhand drive in which a great deal of body weight was put behind the shot. The racket points away from the direction in which the ball was hit.

one in which the ball has been hit.
- Where the forearm is greatly exerted in the hitting phase, the racket may be tilted towards the right in a windscreen wiper-type action
- With the extreme backhand grip and the resulting very early point of impact, the movement of the arm in the follow-through phase is continued upwards, with the angle between the forearm and the racket remaining virtually constant.

Common mistakes

The backswing phase
- Using the centre forehand grip
The face of the racket can't, as a result, be positioned upright, making hitting the ball with full force impossible.
- Little or no turning of the upper body and excessively short backswing action
This makes it impossible to accelerate your racket sufficiently.
- Failing to support the backswing action with the left hand
This often means that your upper body isn't turned far enough back and your movement contol, particularly on the transition between the backswing and hitting phase, suffers as a result; this mistake can become a fault if the left arm moves against the right arm in the backswing phase.
- Little bending of the legs
This too impedes the acceleration of your racket.
- No marked sideways-on position
This leads to a shortening of your backswing.

The striking phase
- Failing to lower the head of the racket
Not taking your racket below the subsequent point of impact prevents you from swinging your racket steeply forwards and upwards.
- Straightening the legs too early

Early straightening of the right leg on hitting indicates poor movement co-ordination.

This affects your co-ordination of the overall movement.
● Abandoning the sideways-on position too early
If your whole body turns with the hitting action it leads to inaccuracy in meeting the ball.
● Little acceleration of the racket
Particularly failing to accelerate the tip of the racket gives the ball insufficient topspin.
● Meeting the ball very late or too far away from the body
These mistakes also lead to an inadequate acceleration of your racket.
● Wrist not firm on meeting the ball
This greatly impairs your control on impact.

The follow-through phase
● Extremely short follow-through movement as a result of interrupting movement
This is an indication that the racket's momentum was decelerated even before the point of impact, or was inadequate in the first place.

TWO-HANDED TOPSPIN BACKHAND

The two-handed topspin backhand drive is used in the same situations and for the same reasons as the single-handed version. The most important features of the two-handed topspin backhand drive concern the following points:
● At the start of the backswing phase your racket should be held with your right hand in a backhand grip and with your left hand in a forehand grip, frequently with the extreme forehand grip.
● In the two-handed grip the head of the racket in the transition between the

backswing and hitting phase is often taken lower than in the single-handed version. Most importantly, this enables the tip of the racket to be swung steeply upwards in the hitting phase to achieve the pronounced topspin. In practice, therefore, comparable players with a two-handed backhand achieve a greater topspin than players who hit the ball with a single-handed stroke.
● As a result of both hands firmly holding the handle of the racket the upper body is forced to turn in the direction in which the ball is to be hit while still in the hitting phase, whereas in a single-handed topspin backhand the body has to remain in the sideways-on position for longer.

Two-handed topspin backhand drive.

Slicing

In which situations and positions is this technique used, and what are its uses and results?
What effects does it have on the ball's behaviour?

Court positions

Sliced forehand and backhand drives are generally played from the baseline area and from the area between the service line and the baseline. The slice is played much more often on the backhand side than on the forehand side.

Tactical uses

● To keep the ball reliably in play.
● Where possible, to play the ball to bounce close to your opponent's baseline (1); this forces your opponent to remain behind the baseline.
● The more shortly played slice, in particular, should bounce low and force your opponent to play it at a disadvantageous, low point (3).
● A service is often returned with a slice (2). In response to a first service it is used because of the need for time and reliability, and in the case of the second service, when the ball is to be played in front of the attacking player's feet.
● A slice helps to vary the ball exchange tempo, to destroy your opponent's rhythm.
● Balls that are only just reached or that have to be played under pressure can still be returned relatively reliably and accurately with a slice.

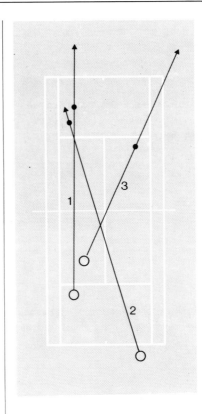

The slice can be used as an attacking shot (1), as a service return (2), and to force an opponent to meet the ball low (3).

● Where your opponent's ball has come too short, it offers an opportunity to attack; this attacking shot is often played as a slice as:
– the ball can be advantageously played in the upward curve
– body movements can be harmoniously combined with the easy hitting action, providing smooth transition with the forward run
– the relatively slow flight of the ball allows you to take up a favourable position at the net.
● High-bouncing balls can be returned in the upward curve as a slice, to prevent you from being forced too far back.

Effects on the ball's behaviour

● The ball hit with a marked backward spin follows a low flight path.
● It generally travels at average speed.
● It bounces relatively low.

The slice travels with a marked backward spin either, where possible, over the service line (1, 2) or short, across the court (3), in all cases with a relatively low flight curve.

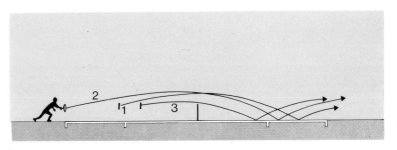

Backswing *The upper body is turned back, the racket taken backwards and upwards, and the left foot brought forward in the direction of hitting.*

Striking the ball *The racket movement is in a flat forwards and downwards curve, with the upper body turning in the direction of the*

1   2   3   4   5   6

FOREHAND SLICE

Basic techniques

This section shows you what you have to do to make the ball do as you intend.

Meeting the ball

● You bring your racket forwards and down in a shallow loop, as shown in photographs 4 to 8, to achieve backward spin.
● You accelerate your racket towards the point of impact to achieve the necessary speed of hitting for the desired spin.
● You swing your racket as far as possible in the direction of hitting to achieve the greatest accuracy and reliability.
● You play the ball with a firm wrist and with your racket face approximately upright, to the side and in front of your body (as shown in photograph 8), to achieve the necessary powerful stroke.

shot. The weight is shifted onto the leading leg, the legs are bent, and the ball played to the side in front of the body with the wrist firm.

Follow-through *The racket initially continues forwards and downwards, then turns forwards and upwards.*

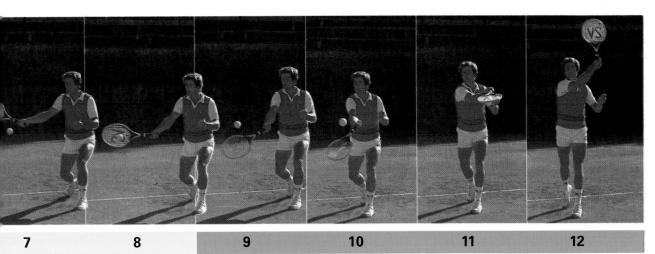

| 7 | 8 | 9 | 10 | 11 | 12 |

The backswing phase

- For the sliced forehand drive you hold your racket in the forehand grip.
- Your upper body and right leg are turned towards the right; you take your racket backwards and upwards (see photgraphs 1 and 2).
- At the end of the backswing movement your right arm is slightly bent, with your upper arm a relatively long way from your upper body. Your racket face is approximately upright, and the racket is above head height, as in photograph 2.
- You bring your left leg, which takes your weight during the hitting and follow-through movements, forward at the end of the backswing phase in the intended direction of hitting (photograph 3); your feet should be wider apart than the width of your hips to give good balance.

The striking phase

- The transition from the backswing to the hitting phase takes the form of a shallow arc, to ensure a smooth sequence of movements, as shown in photographs 3 to 5.
- You transfer your weight forwards and downwards onto your leading leg, bending your legs (as in photographs 4 to 8); this assists the hitting action.
- You turn your upper body in the direction of hitting (see photographs 7 and 8); this is also to assist the hitting action.

The follow-through phase

- The follow-through initially continues forwards and downwards (see photographs 9 and 10); this is an indication that the ball has been given the right backward spin.
- The follow-through then finishes forwards and upwards, with your racket face being opened up increasingly; at the end of the follow-through movement the racket should be at or above head height (see photographs 11 and 12).

FOREHAND SLICE

Acceptable variations

The backswing phase
• Many players adopt the central grip for the sliced forehand drive: this is an advantage for a low point of impact where the face of your racket needs to be slightly open; with a high point of impact, however, this grip is a disadvantage as it makes it very difficult to bring your racket face into an upright position at the point of impact.
• The height and width of the backswing movement can vary; a shorter, flatter backswing movement makes it possible with fast oncoming balls still to begin the hitting action in good time; extremely wide and high backswing movements admittedly enable the hitting speed to be increased, but they also entail the risk of reducing your ball control.
• The flat arc in the transition from the backswing to the hitting movement can be omitted; in certain situations this can lead to better control over the stroke, but your rhythm, flow of movement and racket acceleration suffer as a result.
• The timing/dynamics of the movement can also vary between individuals, particularly in the transition from taking the racket back in the backswing phase and accelerating it in the hitting phase; an extremely early backswing retarded at the end of the backswing movement allows you a leisurely hitting action; if the backswing is late

your transition into the hitting action is smoother, but it may be less well controlled.

The striking phase
• With fast oncoming balls (from a first service, for example) a greatly shortened hitting action, sometimes also directed steeply forwards and downwards, has to be used because of the time pressure; this technique was also previously known as the chop.
• A hitting movement from right to left in front of the body gives the ball additional sidespin. This enables you to play balls played into your body as slice strokes.

The follow-through phase
• The more leisurely and the longer the hitting movement, the longer too is the follow-through movement.
• With a short hitting action the follow-through upwards can be so short as to be barely perceptible.
• In certain situations (the return of a slow service, a passing shot played short across court, an attacking shot from the centre of the court, for instance) the follow-through upwards can also be shortened.
• In a slice with additional sidespin the follow-through is shorter and goes to the top left.

Common mistakes

The backswing phase
• Using the backhand grip
This results in the face of your racket not being upright at the ideal point of impact.
• Little or no turning of the upper body
This shortens the backswing movement and hitting becomes a punching action or the racket swings to the left in front of your body.
• Late backswing movement
The required leisurely hitting action is no longer possible in this case.
• Tight backswing
This brings your upper arm too close to your body, leading to a punching action.
• Swinging straight backwards
This means the hitting movement can't be made from the top downwards, and the ball isn't given the backward spin you want.

The striking phase
• Failing to bend the front leg
This means that there is no transfer of your weight forwards and down to assist the stroke.
• Abandoning the sideways-on hitting position early, and early inward turn of the hip and upper body
This leads to the hitting action taking place to the left in front of your body, and your accuracy in meeting the ball suffers as a result.
• Wrist not firm on meeting the ball
This seriously hampers your

Not bending the left leg on hitting means you can't assist the hitting action in a forwards and downwards direction.

A wide open racket face at the point of impact causes the ball to fly off high with little speed.

control of impact with the ball.
● Wide open racket face on meeting the ball
This means that the ball is not given sufficient speed, and flies away too high.
● Meeting the ball too late
This severely shortens the hitting action and the ball can't be given sufficient spin or speed.

The follow-through phase
● Early abrupt ending of the follow-through movement
This indicates poor control over the ball
● Bending the arm too much
This results in you taking the racket to your left shoulder too early and again indicates poor ball control.

Meeting the ball too late means the ball isn't given sufficient spin or speed.

Early, pronounced bending of the arm on hitting leads to an uncontrolled hitting action.

Follow-through *The racket initially continues forwards and downwards, then finishes forwards and upwards.*

Striking the ball *The racket moves flatly forwards and downwards, the body weight is shifted onto the front leg and the legs moved into a*

| 14 | 13 | 12 | 11 | 10 | 9 | 8 |

BACKHAND SLICE

Basic techniques

This section shows you what you have to do to make the ball do as you intend.

Meeting the ball

● The racket movement is flat from top back to bottom front, to give a backward spin.
● You accelerate your racket towards the point of impact to achieve the necessary hitting speed for the spin you want to give.
● Swing your racket as far as possible in the direction of hitting, to achieve a high degree of accuracy and reliability.
● Play the ball with a firmly braced wrist and with your racket face approximately upright, to the side in front of your body (between photographs 9 and 10) to achieve the most effective transfer of force.

The backswing phase

● You hold the racket in the backhand grip for the sliced backhand.
● Turn your upper body and left leg to the left (your upper body is turned farther back than in the sliced forehand drive), and take your racket backwards and upwards, as in photograph 2.
● Keep your left hand on the neck of the racket in the backswing movement (photographs 1 to 6) so that the backswing action can be stabilized and your upper body turned further back.
● At the end of the backswing movment your arm should be well bent, your upper arm well away from your body, your racket face well open (almost parallel to the ground), and your racket head at shoulder height, as shown in photograph 6.

sideways-on position. The ball is played to the side in front of the body with a firmly braced wrist.

Backswing *There is a pronounced turning of the upper body, the racket is taken backwards and upwards supported by the left hand,*

with the racket face well open and the right leg is brought forward in the direction of the shot.

7   6   5   4   3   2   1

The striking phase

The follow-through phase

• Your right leg, which takes your weight in the hitting and follow-through movement, should be brought forward during the backswing phase into the intended direction of the shot; your feet should be more than your hips' width apart to give you good balance.

• The backswing movement has a flat upper arc to give a smooth transition into the hitting phase; the loop is smaller than in the sliced forehand drive.
• Shift your weight forwards and downwards onto your leading leg, with your legs bent: this assists the direction of the hitting action, as shown in photographs 7 to 10.
• Fully extend your right arm during the hitting movement to achieve an ideal point of impact. At the same time, turn your forearm so that your racket face can be positioned approximately upright at the point of impact for the most effective stroke (photographs 7 to 10).
• Maintain your sideways-on foot and body position as far as the point of impact and beyond, as shown in photographs 7 to 12.

• The follow-through initially continues further forwards and downwards, as shown in photographs 10 to 12, which demonstrates that the ball has been given adequate spin.
• The follow-through then ends forwards and upwards, with your racket face being opened up increasingly: at the end of the follow-through movement the hand holding your racket should be at shoulder height, as in photographs 13 and 14.

BACKHAND SLICE

Acceptable variations

The backswing phase

● Many players adopt the central grip for the sliced backhand drive. This is an advantage for a low point of impact, where the face of the racket needs to be slightly open; but with a high point of impact this grip is a handicap as it makes it very difficult to bring your racket face into an upright position at the point of impact. Essentially, it's difficult in the sliced backhand to hit the ball with full force using the central grip.

● The height and width of the backswing movement can vary; turning the body slightly and lifting the elbow slightly, at least associated with a lower backswing movement, admittedly allows the racket to be brought to the point of impact in good time with a fast oncoming ball, but the smoothness and momentum of the movement suffer as a result. A wide, high backswing action – with the body turned considerably, and the elbow taken well back and raised, the right hand close to the left shoulder – allows you to hit the ball with considerable momentum and at high speed, although with some loss of control.

● The timing/dynamics of the movement can vary between individuals, particularly in the transition from taking back the racket in the backswing phase and its acceleration in the hitting phase; taking it back very early, decelerating the movement at the end of the backswing phase allows a leisurely hitting action: if the backswing is late the transition from the backswing to the hitting action may be smoother, but it may also possibly be less controlled.

● The backswing is often shorter in a slice with additional sidespin, and starts from the top right.

The striking phase

● With fast oncoming balls (from a first service, for instance) a considerably shortened hitting action, in some cases directed steeply forwards and downwards, may be used because of limited time: this technique used to be known as the chop.

● The hitting movement is

from left to right, giving the ball additional sidespin. This enables balls played into the body to be played as slice strokes.

● Players often differ in the part of the hitting action in which they extend their racket arm; reaching out only shortly before the point of impact increases the speed of the stroke and promotes meeting the ball very early; this does, however, make ball control difficult; much earlier stretching of the arm limits the stroke speed.

The follow-through phase

● The more leisurely and the longer the hitting movement, the longer too is the follow-through movement.

Backswing for a sliced backhand with the elbow well raised; the racket hand is around shoulder height giving a wide backswing action.

Backswing for a sliced backhand with the elbow slightly less raised than usual in a flat backswing action. The elbow can be held even lower.

In the sliced backhand drive the hitting arm remains bent for some time, and is only extended just before the point of impact.

In this example of a sliced backhand the hitting arm is extended at an early stage.

• With a short hitting action the follow-through upwards can be so short as to be barely perceptible.
• In certain situations (as in a return of a slow service, a passing shot played short across court, an attacking shot from the centre of the court), the follow-through upwards can also be shortened.

Common mistakes

The backswing phase

• Using the forehand grip
This results in the face of your racket not being upright at the ideal point of impact.
• Little or no turning of the upper body
The restricted backswing movement which results means that your hitting action is no longer in the direction of the shot, but to the right of it.
• Late backswing movement
This makes the required leisurely hitting action impossible and the ball is frequently no longer met in good time.

• Long armed backswing
This makes it impossible to accelerate your racket sufficiently and difficult to maintain your sideways-on position.

The striking phase

• Failing to bend the front leg
This means that there is no transfer of your weight forwards and downwards to assist the stroke.
• Abandoning the sideways-on position early
This means that your body turns with the hitting action and as a result your impact with the ball is uncontrolled.
• Wrist not firm on meeting the ball
This has a serious adverse effect on your control of impact with the ball and lessens the force behind the stroke.
• Wide open racket face on meeting the ball
This leads to the ball not being given sufficient speed, and it will fly away too high.
• Failing to extend the arm sufficiently during the hitting action.
• Meeting the ball too late
This results in the hitting action and follow-through being severely shortened.

The follow-through phase

• Early deviation of the follow-through movement from the direction of the shot.
• Failing to complete the follow-through movement forwards and upwards
To stop the momentum nonetheless, the wrist is often pushed forward, and the racket often also tips away, down to the right.

Lobbing

In which situations and positions is the technique used, and what are its uses and results?
What effects does it have on the ball's behaviour?

Court positions

The lob is generally played from the baseline area, but sometimes also from the area between the baseline and the service line.

Tactical uses

● To play the ball high over an opponent who is rushing towards or standing at the net.
● To hit the ball in such a way that it bounces as close as possible to the baseline.
● It can also be used as a response to a lob from your opponent following an attack of yours at the net, or to a lob from an opponent remaining at the baseline.
● The straight lob can be played (particularly as a high shot) when seeking to disturb your opponent's rhythm, or to obtain short-term relief from pressure from your opponent.
● The sliced lob is played in particular when you are under pressure and when time is short, i.e. with low, fast balls; the object is to gain time.
● A topspin lob forehand is a particularly good shot if the lob can be played from a good hitting position and (in the case of poor attack from your opponent) the ball is not too low, as it bounces away very fast in your opponent's court after the initial bounce. (Topspin=T).

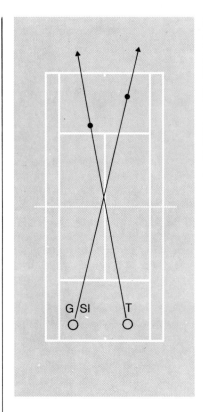

The straight lob (G) and sliced lob (Sl) are generally played from the baseline area, with the topspin lob (T) sometimes being played from the centre part of the court. Where possible the ball should fly to the opposite baseline, making it difficult for an opponent to hit the ball.

*The topspin lob (T) drops sharply and quickly bounces away.
The sliced lob (Sl) drops very sharply close to the opponent's baseline, and bounces away high.
The straight lob (G) should bounce as close as possible to the opponent's baseline.*

Effect on the ball's behaviour

● To play over your opponent the ball should travel neither too low, to prevent your opponent from countering with a smash, nor too high, to prevent your opponent from running to it, as a result of the time then available.
● When used as a defensive shot or as a ball difficult to counter with a smash (particularly against the sun), the ball's flight should be as high as possible.
● The straight lob should fly without any pronounced forward or backward spin.
● The sliced lob should fly with a pronounced backward spin, and as far as possible should drop steeply.
● The topspin lob should fly with a pronounced forward spin and should bounce away quickly after the initial bounce.

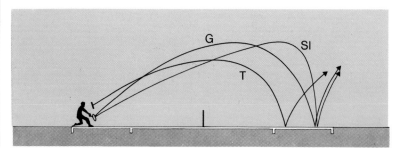

Backswing *The upper body is turned and the racket taken back in the upper arc, and the weight shifted onto the right leg.*

Striking the ball *The left leg is brought forward in the direction of the stroke and the racket lowered and swung steeply forwards and upwards; at the same time the*

| 1 | 2 | 3 | 4 | 5 | 6 |

STRAIGHT LOB

Basic techniques

This section shows you what you have to do to make the ball do as you intend.

Meeting the ball

- You swing your racket steeply forwards and upwards with the racket face open, as in photographs 7 to 9.
- Swing your racket as far as possible in the direction of the shot, as in photographs 7 to 9, to achieve sound accuracy and reliability.
- Swing your racket with less acceleration than for the ground stroke to achieve greater accuracy and reliability.
- You should meet the ball to the side and in front of your hip with your wrist firm and your racket face open, as shown in photograph 9, to achieve ideal impact force.

The backswing phase

- At the start of the backswing phase you should hold your racket in the forehand grip (or with the backhand grip in the straight backhand lob) so that the ball can be met far enough in front of your body.
- In the straight backhand lob, you also begin the backswing movement by taking the racket back by the neck in your left hand; this stabilizes the backswing movement and causes your upper body to turn further backwards.
- Turn your upper body towards the right (in the straight backhand lob to the left).
- Take your racket back with a pronounced upper arc, particularly in the straight forehand lob (as in photographs 3 and 4), to allow a smooth transition into the hitting phase.

weight is transferred onto the left leg. The ball is played to the side and in front of the hip, with a firmly-braced wrist and the face of the racket open.

Follow-through *The racket moves sharply upwards, and a relatively long way in the direction of the shot.*

| 7 | 8 | 9 | 10 | 11 | 12 |

The striking phase

- Shift your centre of gravity downwards by deeply bending the knees, as shown in photographs 5 and 6.
- Bring you left leg (or the right leg in the straight backhand lob), which will be taking your weight in the hitting and follow-through movement, forward in the intended direction of the shot (see photograph 5); your feet should be at least your hips' width apart, but preferably wider, to improve your balance.
- Lower your racket sharply in the transition to the hitting phase, and open it, particularly in the straight backhand lob, so that you will be able to swing it with the racket face in the ideal position for the point of impact.
- Transfer you body weight onto your front leg (see photographs 5 to 8).

- Begin to straighten your legs to assist the upwards movement, co-ordinating with the main action.
- Keep your racket arm reaching out sideways.
- Maintain your sideways-on foot position in the forehand and backhand lob. In the forehand lob you turn your upper body in the direction of the shot. In the backhand lob you maintain the sideways-on position so you can meet the ball at the ideal point of impact and achieve good control over your stroke.

The follow-through phase

- The momentum of your racket's movement carries it a relatively long way in the direction of the shot and sharply upwards, as shown in photographs 10 to 12.
- At the end of the follow-through movement your racket should be well above head height, as in photograph 12.

STRAIGHT LOB

Acceptable variations

The backswing phase
● Many players (as in the ground strokes) use the centre grip for the straight forehand and backhand lob, too; this is not a handicap mainly because the acceleration of movement and power being the stroke in the straight lob are not as significant in meeting the ball.
● The loop, particularly, and the timing/dynamics of the movement vary between individuals, especially in the transition between taking back the racket in the backswing phase and its upwards movement in the hitting phase.
● If you mean to mislead your opponent as to the shot that you're about to play, so that he

expects a ground stroke, for example, the backswing can be similar to that in a ground stroke.

The striking phase
● In many cases the hitting action is carried out with the upper body leaning backwards: this can be beneficial with a fast oncoming ball, as it gains time, and assists the sharp upward movement of the racket.

The follow-through phase
● The slower the hitting action, the shorter the follow-through movement, too, can be.

Common mistakes

The backswing phase
● Little or no turning of the upper body
This limits the breadth of your backswing movement. Also, in a backhand lob, it means you can't make a loose swinging movement in the hitting phase.
● Failing to bend the knees
If you do this the support for the sharp upwards movement of the racket in the main action is lacking, and in particular the timing/dynamics of the total movement and co-ordination of all the individual movements are adversely affected.
● Failing to assist the backswing movement with the left hand in the straight

backhand lob
As a result of this error your upper body is often not turned back sufficiently, and your movement control, particularly on the transition between the backswing and hitting phase, is hindered.

The hitting phase
● Failing to take the racket head low enough
This handicaps you in the steep upward movement of your racket.
● Straightening the legs too early
This inhibits the co-ordination of your forward and upward swing
● Meeting the ball very late, too far from or too close to the body
These mistakes also lead to poor stroke control.
● Wrist not firm on meeting the ball
This has a serious effect on your control of the ball.

The follow-through phase
● Ending the follow-through very early
By cutting off the flow of movement with a slow oncoming ball you seriously affect your control of the ball.
● Decelerating the movement immediately after the point of impact
This demonstrates that the impetus of the hitting action and ball control were faulty.

Failing to take the head of the racket down low at the start of the hitting action makes it impossible to achieve the required sharp upward movement of the racket towards the point of impact.

Follow-through *The racket continues way forward and up.*

Striking the ball *With the knees well bent, the racket is swung flatly forwards and downwards with the face of the racket well open,*

| 10 | 9 | 8 | 7 | 6 |

SLICED LOB

Basic techniques

This section shows you what you have to do to make the ball do as you intend.

Meeting the ball

• You swing your racket, particularly the head of the racket, flatly forwards and upwards and with the racket face well open, as in photographs 5 and 6, so that the ball can be hit in a steep flight path, with backward spin.

• You should meet the ball to the side and, particularly in the backhand sliced lob, in front of your hip with your wrist firmly braced and with your racket face well open, (as in photograph 6) to achieve the most powerful shot.

The backswing phase

• At the start of the backswing phase in the sliced backhand lob you hold your racket in the backhand grip (or in the sliced forehand lob in the forehand grip) so that the ball can be met far enough in front of your body and the force with which you hit the ball can be increased.

• In the sliced backhand lob the backswing movement is begun by your left hand taking the racket back by the neck (as in photographs 1 and 2) to stabilize the backswing movement and allow your upper body to be turned further backwards.

• Turn your upper body towards the back (more sharply in the backhand than in the forehand), taking your racket back in a flat upper arc.

• Open up the face of your racket in the transition to the hitting phase (photographs 2 to 4), so that the ideal position of the racket face is reached at *meeting the ball to the side and in front of the hip, and with the racket face well open and the wrist firmly braced.*

Backswing *The upper body is turned and the racket taken back in a flat upper arc, and the weight is transferred onto the right leg.*

5   4   3   2   1

The striking phase

The follow-through phase

the point of impact.
● You bring your right leg (or the left leg in the sliced forehand lob), which takes your weight in the hitting and follow-through movements, forward in the intended direction of the shot (see photographs 1 and 2). To improve your balance your feet should be at least your hips' width apart. In the sliced backhand lob the sideways-on position is so pronounced that the back of your right shoulder points towards the net.

● Transfer your body weight onto your leading leg and lower your centre of gravity by deeply bending your knees (as in photographs 3 to 6); this is done to assist the downward movement of your racket.
● In the sliced backhand lob your right arm should be straight during the main action, as in photograph 4; this is related to the fact that your racket arm is in front of your body and was sharply bent at the elbow in the backswing; in the forehand sliced lob, your arm should already be extended at the beginning of the main action; in both techniques your wrist should remain relatively firm throughout the main action.

● Your racket swings well forwards and upwards (higher than in the sliced forehand and backhand drives) as shown in photographs 8 to 10; this demonstrates that the ball has been given the proper spin, and that sufficient momentum has been transferred to it.
● The follow-through movement forwards and upwards is assisted by straightening your front leg, as in photographs 9 and 10.

SLICED LOB

Acceptable variations

The backswing phase
• Many players hit the forehand and backhand sliced lob with the centre grip: this is not a disadvantage, mainly because the face of the racket is not brought into an upright position on meeting the ball.
• The loop, particularly, and the timing/dynamics of the movement vary between individuals, especially in the transition between the backswing phase and the hitting phase.
• In the sliced backhand lob the arm may be bent to a greater or lesser degree.

The striking phase
• The main action can be started very late in an attempt to mislead an opponent as to the stroke which you are intending to play, so that your opponent expects a ground stroke, for example.
• If the arm was sharply bent in the sliced backhand lob backswing phase, it may not be at full stretch until just before the point of impact.

The follow-through phase
• The more time a player can take for the hitting action and the more he strives for a long main action, the longer the follow-through movement.

Common mistakes

The backswing phase
• Little or no turning of the upper body
This limits the breadth of your backswing movement. Also, in a sliced backhand lob, it makes it impossible to make a loose swinging movement in the hitting phase.
• Failing to assist the backswing movement with the left hand in the sliced backhand lob
As a result your upper body is often not turned back sufficiently, and your movement control, particularly on the transition between the backswing and hitting phase, is impaired.

The striking phase
• Straightening the legs
This has a bad effect on the direction of the hitting movement.
• Leaning backwards
This prevents your weight from being transferred onto your front leg on hitting,

leading in turn to a weaker hitting action.
• Early movement out of the sideways-on position
If your entire body pivots on the stroke your control of the stroke suffers considerably.
• Meeting the ball very late, or too far from or too close to the body
These mistakes also lead to a lack of reliability and control over your stroke.
• Wrists not firm on meeting the ball
This greatly impairs your control of the ball.
• Failing to straighten the arm on meeting the ball
This indicates a deceleration in the momentum of your hitting action.

The follow-through phase
• Ending the follow-through movement very early
Cutting off the flow of movement abruptly greatly impairs your control of the ball; in addition, insufficient momentum is transferred to it and its flight path is short as a result.

Leaning backwards on meeting the ball shows that the hitting movement has not been assisted by a shift of weight.

71

Backswing *The upper body is turned and the racket taken back in the upper arc, with the weight being transferred onto the right leg.*

Striking the ball *The racket head is taken down low, the racket swung sharply forwards and upwards, with an explosive straightening of the push-off leg with the upper body*

turning, the ball is played to the side and in front of the hip, with the racket face upright and the wrist firmly braced.

1   2   3   4   5

TOPSPIN LOB

Basic techniques

This section shows you what you have to do to make the ball do as you intend.

Meeting the ball

- Swing your racket, particularly the head of the racket, forwards and particularly sharply upwards against the ball (as shown in photographs 5 to 7), to achieve the steep trajectory and pronounced forward spin you want.
- The movement of your racket must be extremely fast for the ball to obtain the required pronounced forward spin.
- You should meet the ball to the side and in front of your leading hip with your wrist firm and the racket face upright (between photographs 6 and 7).

The backswing phase

- At the start of the backswing phase you should hold your racket in the forehand grip (or in the backhand grip for the topspin backhand lob) so that the racket face can be brought into the upright position on meeting the ball, and power can be transferred in the most effective way.
- In the topspin backhand lob the backswing movement is begun with your left hand taking the racket back by the neck to stabilize the backswing movement and allow your upper body to turn further backwards.
- In the topspin forehand lob transfer your weight onto your right leg, which is used as the push-off or bracing leg in the hitting movement, by a turning step to the side (as in photograph 1); the hitting position is open. In the topspin backhand lob, you should take up a full sideways-on position.

Follow-through *The racket continues sharply upwards to well above head height.*

| 6 | 7 | 8 | 9 | 10 |

● Pivot your upper body backwards (particularly sharply in the backhand), taking your racket back in the upper arc (as in photographs 1 and 2), which provides a smooth transition to the hitting phase.
● Lower your centre of gravity by bending your knees deeply and shifting your weight onto your right leg (in the topspin backhand and forehand lob), as shown in photograph 2.

The striking phase

● Take the head of your racket down very low at the start of the hitting phase (photographs 3 to 5), so that you can swing the tip of the racket, particularly, steeply upwards in the hitting phase.
● Begin rising smartly onto the balls of your feet right from the transition from the backswing to the hitting phase in the topspin forehand lob, to assist the sharp upwards movement, with your right leg

pushing off powerfully from the ground (photographs 4 to 6). In the backhand, you rise onto the balls of your feet less explosively and so rather later than in the forehand.
● Turn your upper body forwards in the topspin forehand lob simultaneously with the hitting action so that you can swing your racket not only sharply upwards but also slightly forwards to maximise the power behind your shot.
● In the backhand topspin lob, continue to shift your body weight onto your leading leg, turn your upper body only slightly and maintain the sideways-on position of your feet and body beyond the point of impact to give you sound control and accuracy with your stroke.
● In the topspin forehand and backhand lob, however, you should lean backwards slightly (particularly when compared with a normal topspin): this will enable you to make the steep upward swing even where the point of impact with the ball is high.

The follow-through phase

● The follow-through movement should continue sharply forwards and upwards, as shown in photographs 8 to 10. As a result your racket follows through, and you are guaranteed that the ball has been given a good forward spin.
● At the end of the follow-through movement your racket should be well above head height, as in photograph 10.

TOPSPIN LOB

Acceptable variations

The backswing phase
- Individuals may vary in their forehand or backhand grip.
- The loop, particularly, and the timing/dynamics of the movement vary between individuals, especially in the transition between taking the racket back in the backswing phase and its upward movement in the hitting phase.

The racket swings right behind the back at the beginning of the topspin lob.

Follow-through here is a windscreen wiper-type action, in front of the body, to the left.

The striking phase
- The topspin forehand lob can also be played with the arm fully extended, in which case the arm is twisted to accelerate the head of the racket.
- The extent of the backward lean in the hitting phase can vary; a pronounced backward lean helps the vertical upwards movement of the racket.

Topspin forehand lob with a straight arm, the arm being twisted inwards to accelerate the racket head.

The follow-through phase
- The more momentum in the hitting action, the longer the follow-through movement.
- The racket can be followed through over the racket shoulder so that the racket ends up behind the back; this applies particularly when the point of impact is low and rather late.
- With pronounced exertion of the forearm and a very early point of impact, follow-through is to the left in a windscreen wiper-type action.

Common mistakes

Failing to lower the head of your racket sufficiently at the start of the hitting action means you can't make the sharp upward movement to the point of impact.

The backswing phase

● Lack of pronounced forehand or backhand grip
This stops you from making the most powerful shot possible.
● Exaggerated sideways-on position in the topspin forehand lob
This makes your weight shift and the bending of your right leg difficult and affects the pivoting of your upper body in the hitting phase.
● Lack of pronounced sideways-on position in the topspin backhand lob
This leads to a foreshortened backswing movement.
● Little or no rotation of the upper body
This limits the breadth of your backswing movement and therefore the subsequent acceleration of your racket.
● Failing to support the backswing movement with the left hand in the topspin backhand lob
This frequently means that your upper body is not turned sufficiently towards the back, and your movement control, particularly on the transition between the backswing and hitting phase is hampered.
● Failing to bend the knees sufficiently
This too results in poor acceleration of movement.

The striking phase

● Failing to lower the head of the racket sufficiently at the start of the hitting phase.
● Rising on your toes too soon.

This upsets your co-ordination of the movement as a whole.
● Moving out of the sideways-on position too soon in the topspin backhand lob
If your entire body twists with the hitting action in the direction of the shot it greatly impairs your control over the stroke.
● Little acceleration of the racket, particularly the tip of the racket
As a result of this the ball isn't given sufficient forward spin.
● Meeting the ball very late, or too far from or too close to the body
These mistakes too lead to poor ball control.
● Wrist not firm on meeting the ball
This severely impairs your control on impact.

The follow-through phase

● Ending the sharp upward movement very early by abruptly halting your movement
This demonstrates that you didn't have enough momentum, or that you slowed it before the point of impact.

Serving

In which situations and positions is this technique used, and what are its uses and results?
What effects does it have on the ball's behaviour?

Court positions

The service is played as the opening shot from behind the baseline, and depending on the state of play, from right or left.

Tactical uses

• On a first service possibly to make an immediate point, in which case the ball is played primarily over the centre of the net (1).
• To put your opponent under pressure with the speed and precision of the ball, so that he is forced to make a weak or faulty return.
• To play a second service mainly for reliability and place-ment, as any failed attempt will mean losing a point.
• Often the straight service is used on a first service and a slice service or twist service as the second service.
• A sliced service from the right to your opponent's forehand side should be played in such a way as to force him sideways out of his position. The effects of sidespin on the sliced service as it bounces are more unpleasant for your opponent the smoother the ground. It is therefore used primarily in indoor games (3).
• A twist service is generally played from the left side onto your opponent's backhand to

force him sideways out of position and to compel him to play the ball at a high point of impact, as this service flies away high after bouncing (2).
• The effects of forward spin on the bounce are all the more unpleasant for your opponent the rougher the ground, as the effect of the spin is particularly marked here.

Effects on the ball's behaviour

• The ball should fly in a flat curve at high speed in the straight service (1).
• In the sliced service the ball should fly in a flat trajectory, with a more marked sidespin than forward spin.
• In the twist service it should fly over the net in a high and sharply curved path, with marked forward spin.

The straight service (1) flies over the net relatively flat at high speed.
The twist service (2) has a higher flight path, a marked forward spin, and bounces fast and high.
The slice service (3) travels at average speed, has more sidespin than topspin, and seen from the server's end, descends to the left.

A first service (1) designed to gain a direct point is generally played over the centre of the net.
The twist service (2) is played mainly from the left onto the opponent's backhand side.
A sliced service (3) from the right onto the opponent's forehand is extremely effective, especially on a smooth playing surface.

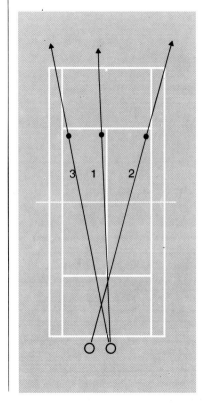

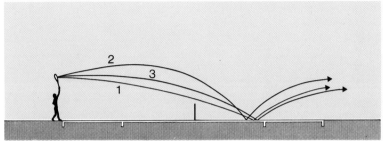

Follow-through *Initially the racket continues to the outside right, then to the left side of the body, with the upper body turned in the direction of* *the shot, the body weight taken onto the right foot and the left arm in front of the body.* **Striking the ball** *With the upper body turned in the direction of the shot, the racket accelerates sharply upwards and forwards. The arm is*

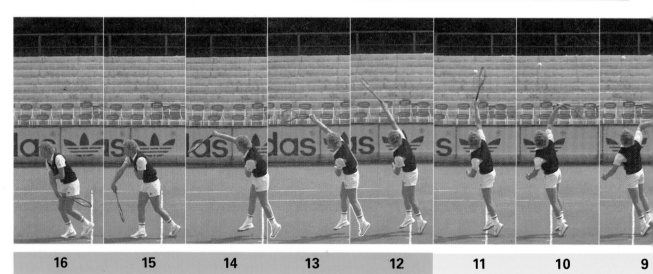

| 16 | 15 | 14 | 13 | 12 | 11 | 10 | 9 |

STRAIGHT SERVICE

Basic techniques

This section shows you what you have to do to make the ball do as you intend.

Meeting the ball

● You accelerate the head of your racket in a sharp upwards and forwards direction to the point of impact with the ball, as shown in photographs 8 to 11.
● The head of your racket should be almost perpendicular to the ground and at right angles to the direction of the shot at the point of impact with the ball (see photograph 11).
● You should hit the ball at a point vertically above the area just in front of your left foot and about 20 cm (8 inches) inside the baseline.

The backswing phase

● Hold your racket in the backhand grip.
● Stand with your legs about shoulders' width apart, as in photograph 1, to give a stable starting position.
● At the start of the backswing phase, first take your racket downwards in the lower arc in a pendulum action, and then backwards and upwards, as in photographs 1 to 3.
● At the same time twist backwards from the waist and temporarily transfer your weight onto your right leg (photographs 1 to 3)
● During the pendulum movement of your racket, you should be bringing your left hand, in which you are holding the ball, upwards.
● Your left arm should move up in the approximate direction of the right hand post of the net for the ball to be thrown to the ideal point of impact.
● The ball should leave your

rotated shortly before meeting the ball so that the palm of the hand points outwards and the point of contact is as high as possible.

Backswing The pendulum action coincides with taking the throwing arm up, the weight shifts onto the front leg, the upper body leans back to arch the body and the racket is taken over the right shoulder.

8 7 6 5 4 3 2 1

hand about level with your forehead (see photograph 3) to give you good control of the height and direction of throwing.
● Throw the ball a little higher than the highest point of impact you could possibly reach.
● At the same time as shifting your weight onto your left leg, lean your upper body backwards, push your pelvis forwards and bend your knees, particularly the left one, as in photographs 4 and 5.
● Lean your upper body increasingly backwards, completing the tension of the arc. The arc tension provides for a long acceleration path, and helps you achieve maximum acceleration in the main action.
● While your knees and pelvis are being pushed forwards, take your racket over your right shoulder by bending your elbow (photographs 4 and 5).

The striking phase

● Stretching your body towards the point of impact starts from the ground upwards: first your knees (photographs 6 and 7), then your upper body (photographs 7 to 9), the arm at the elbow (photographs 9 and 10), and finally your wrist (photograph 11).
● Your racket should reach the lowest point in its loop behind your back only when your legs are straight.
● While reaching up turn your body in the direction of the shot (photographs 8 to 11).
● At the point of impact your right shoulder should be as high as possible, with your left foot, right shoulder and racket hand in a single line, as in photograph 11.
● Your right foot should leave the ground and move forward in the direction of the shot when the racket hits the ball. This makes it possible for you to shift your weight forwards (see photographs 9 to 11).

The follow-through phase

● After the racket has met the ball your right forearm twists further outwards and swings down to the right (photographs 12 and 13).
● Given the considerable acceleration of the racket and the turning of your arm, your wrist tips down forwards and to the right, as in photograph 14.
● Your upper body follows the ball in the direction of the shot.
● Your right foot lands and takes your weight, as shown in photographs 15 and 16.
● Your racket arm follows through in front of your body in the lower arc towards the left side of the body, as in photograph 16.
● Your left arm moves in front of your body, as in photographs 13 to 16.

Backswing *Simultaneous pendulum action of the racket with the throwing arm moving upwards, transferring the weight onto the* *front leg and leaning the upper body backwards with the racket over the right shoulder.*

Striking the ball *Body stretched, racket at the lowest point in the loop, the upper body turned in the direction of the shot (more so in the slice than in the twist), sharp*

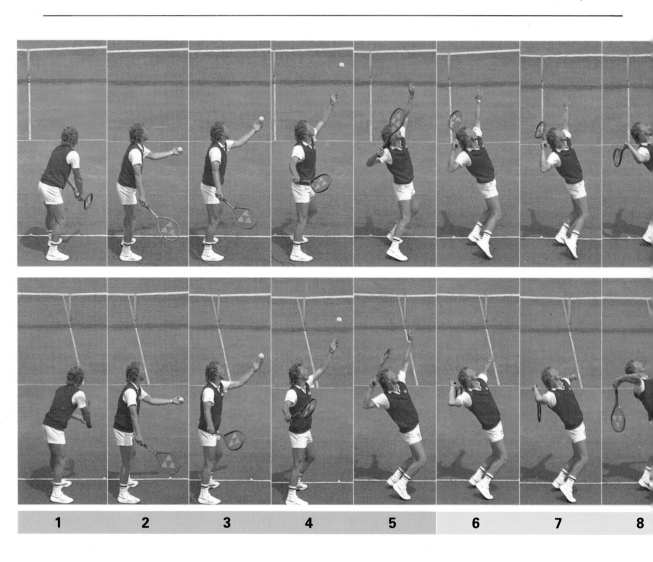

| 1 | 2 | 3 | 4 | 5 | 6 | 7 | 8 |

SLICED AND TWIST SERVICE

Basic techniques

The sliced service is illustrated in the top series of photographs, and the twist service in the bottom series.

Meeting the ball

• Accelerate th head of your racket sharply upwards and forwards behind your back (photographs 9 to 12) to reach it highest speed at the point of impact.
• Depending on the type of stroke being played (slice or twist), swing your racket through the point of impact, either at an angle to the side (slice), as in upper

photographs 11 and 12, or at more of an angle upwards (twist) (as in lower photographs 11 and 12).
• At the point of impact with the ball the head of your racket should be almost perpendicular to the ground and at right angles to the direction of the shot, as in photographs 12, to give the ball the desired trajectory.
• Hit the ball just as it begins to drop from its highest point, at a point vertically above the area just in front of your left

upwards and forwards acceleration of the racket through the point of impact, slightly below the highest point.

Follow-through The racket initially continues outwards and to the right (particularly in the twist), then to the left side of the body, the upper body is turned in the direction of the shot

(in the twist combined with a slight tilt to the left), the weight is on the right foot (slice) or left foot (twist) and the left arm is in front of the body.

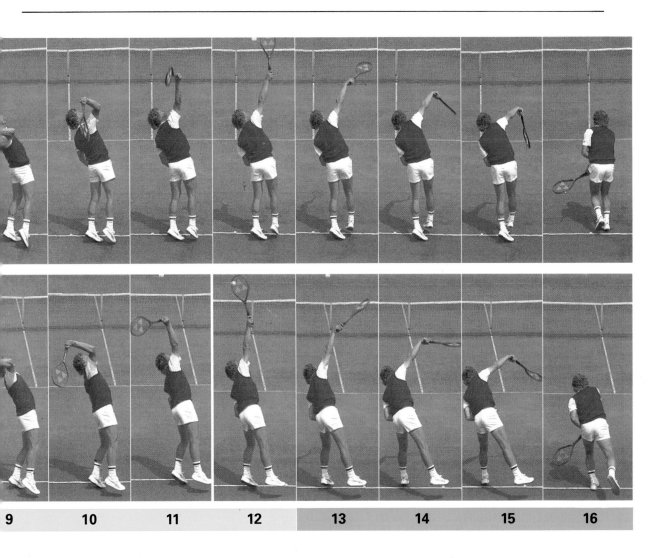

9 10 11 12 13 14 15 16

foot and about 20 cm (8 inches) inside the baseline, to give the forwards and upwards transfer of weight. Depending on the spin combination, however, the ball may be met a little further to the right, as in upper photograph 12 (in the slice) or further to the left, as in lower photograph 12 (in the twist) than in the basic service.

The backswing phase

● Hold your racket in the backhand grip, standing with your feet about shoulders' width apart to give a stable starting position (see photographs 1).
● At the start of the backswing movement first take your racket downwards in the lower arc, then upwards to about shoulder height, as in photographs 1 to 4.

● At the same time turn your upper body backwards and shift your weight briefly onto your right foot (see photographs 1 to 4). The upper body movement is slightly more pronounced in the slice than in the twist.
● With the start of the pendulum action of your racket, simultaneously start the upwards movement of your outstretched left arm, holding the ball with your wrist firm (photographs 2 to 4).
● Move your ball-throwing

SLICED AND TWIST SERVICE

arm up approximately in the direction of the right post of the net, so that the ball can be thrown under proper control to the ideal point of impact (see photographs 4).

● The ball should leave your hand at around forehead height, as in photographs 3, to ensure good control of the direction and height of the throw.

● Throw the ball higher than the highest attainable point of impact.

● As your weight is transferred onto the left foot your upper body begins to lean backwards, as in photographs 5.

● Push your pelvis upwards.

● Bend your knees – particularly the left one.

● Lean your upper body increasingly backwards; this completes the arching action, which is generally greater in the twist service than in the slice service (compare upper and lower photographs 5); among other things, this arching provides a long acceleration path and helps achieve maximum acceleration in the main action.

● As your knees bend take your racket over your right shoulder by bending your elbow (see photographs 5).

The striking phase

● Stretch your body upwards to the point of impact from the bottom upwards, beginning with your legs (see photographs 6 to 9).

● Stretch your upper body upwards and swing your racket out of the lowest point in the loop to the point of impact (photographs 9 to 12).

● While your body is stretching upwards turn from the waist in the direction of the shot: this rotation of your upper body is more pronounced in the sliced service than in the twist service: (compare upper and lower photographs 10 to 12) in the slice your upper body is turned farther to the front than in the twist with your body weight on your left foot.

● In the main action extend your arm fully after your legs and upper body; finally, just before the point of impact, by bending your wrist, swing your racket to the point of impact at high speed.

● Your hitting arm is thus fully extended, and the shoulder of your hitting arm should be as high as possible enabling you to hit the ball at the ideal point. On meeting the ball your left foot, right shoulder and racket hand should be in a straight line, as in photographs 12.

● To help co-ordination and the transfer of weight your right foot lifts off the ground; in the slice, it overtakes your left foot in the main action as a result of the direction of movement of your arm and the relatively sharp forward turn of your upper body (see photographs 10 to 12); in the twist, your right foot moves in the main action in relation to the direction of the hitting action and the relatively slight sideways and backwards turn of your body.

The follow-through phase

● After hitting the ball your right forearm rotates outwards and swings to the right (see photographs 13 and 14). The first part of the follow-through is directed more to the right in the twist than in the slice.

● Given the considerable acceleration of the racket in the main action and the twisting of your arm at the start of the follow-through phase, your wrist tips downwards to the right and forwards, as shown in photographs 14 and 15.

● In the slice service your upper body follows the ball in the direction of the shot (see upper photographs 14 and 15); in the twist service, for reasons of co-ordination and balance, your body initially (with only a slight turn) leans slightly to the left, and then turns in the direction of the shot (see lower photographs 14 and 15).

● In the slice service it is your right foot that lands and takes you body weight, whereas in the twist service it is the left foot (see photographs 15 and 16).

● Your racket arm swings in front of your body in the lower arc to the left side of your body, as shown in photographs 16; this is for reasons of balance and to prevent your body from turning too far.

Acceptable variations

The backswing phase
- Many players use the centre grip; this grip can, however, cause a certain restriction of the movement in your wrist.
- There can be differences in the respective timings of the racket movement and throwing the ball:
  – both arms can be taken down simultaneously, then take up together
  – the downwards movement of the hand holding the ball can be very fast and short
  – the right arm with the racket can be taken downwards and the left arm with the ball taken upwards.

All three methods give a good service; for reasons of co-ordination, the second and third methods are preferable; the height to which the ball is thrown is affected by the timing of the various movements which lead up to the throw.

- Many players take the ball up with the arm slightly bent, but it is better to keep your arm straight to achieve a better control of the throwing action.
- Many players begin the service with the weight on their right leg; this is recommended as long as you don't begin to rise onto your toes prematurely on transferring the weight to your left foot.
- The right foot can be taken forward to a greater or lesser degree; the important thing is not to turn your hips too soon on taking or drawing it forward.
- There can be differences in the direction of throwing; in the slice service many players throw the ball further right and forward, and in the twist service further left and backwards to increase the spin effect in each case; a disadvantage here, however, is

In the service your right foot may be placed in front in the backswing phase, provided that your right hip isn't turned forwards as a result.

SLICED AND TWIST SERVICE

Pronounced backward arching of the body at the end of the backswing movement.

In the twist service (top) the ball is thrown a little further backwards, and in the slice service (below), it is thrown a little further to the right.

that your opponent soon realizes which spin action is being attempted, and the speed of the ball is reduced in favour of spin.

The striking phase

- Individuals generally vary considerably in timing/dynamics.
- The arching of the body and subsequent transfer of weight forwards and up to assist the hitting action can vary between individuals.
- Many players leap into the air with the force of the shot.
- Players differ in their body pivot in the sliced service or back bend in the twist service in relation to the different directions in which they throw the ball to increase the spin

action. There are considerable differences in the use of the body, particularly between large and small players: large players tend to arch their body less.

The follow-through phase
● If very little use is made of the body the right foot may remain behind the baseline after the stroke.
● If a player leaps off the ground in the twist service with the great force of the shot, his right leg swings backwards and to the side to maintain balance and his body weight is taken by his left leg. In the sliced service, the player springs from the left leg onto the right foot, and in the straight service, the body weight may be taken on either the right or the left leg.

The great force behind the service stroke may make a player leave the ground.

SLICED AND TWIST SERVICE

Common mistakes

The backswing phase

● Using the forehand grip
This makes it difficult to stretch your wrist at the point of impact and you won't be able to meet the ball at the highest point.

● Legs too close together in the starting position
This can lead to problems in maintaining your balance.

● Position too frontal
This reduces the momentum that also comes from the rotation of your body.

● No pendulum action
Your racket being raised in front of the body over your right shoulder greatly shortens your backswing action: it also disrupts the rhythm of the movement.

● Bringing the upper arm in towards the upper body on bending the elbow
This interrupts the fluidity of your movement, and reduces acceleration.

● Immediate transfer of body weight onto the front foot
As a result of this your body, too, is generally at full stretch too soon. The proper use of your body is missing, and in addition your upper body is leant forward too soon before meeting the ball.

● Throwing the ball too high
This disturbs the timing/dynamics of your movement, as you have to wait until the ball comes back to the height of impact; it's also difficult to meet a ball with precision when it's dropping vertically and fast.

Bringing the upper arm in towards the upper body on bending the arm interrupts the fluidity and rhythm of the movement.

Stretching the body too early doesn't allow the hitting action to be assisted by the transfer of weight.

● Not throwing the ball high enough
This results in an over-hasty backswing movement and the point of impact doesn't coincide with the moment when your whole body is fully stretched.

● In the straight service, throwing the ball too far to the front, side or rear
As a result your weight is transferred in the wrong direction and the ball isn't met at the ideal point of impact.

● Throwing the ball too far to the left in the sliced service or too far to the right or front in the twist service
This makes it virtually impossible to move your arm in the direction needed to achieve the spin action.

The striking phase

● Breaking the continuous flow of movement at the lowest point in the loop
This makes it impossible to achieve the maximum momentum of the racket at the point of impact and hampers co-ordination.

● Failing to extend the hitting arm fully
As a result the racket has less momentum in meeting the ball, and the ball isn't met at the highest possible point.

● Lowering the weight back onto the right foot
This causes your body to lean back, and the reliability of the stroke suffers as a result as your body isn't being used in the direction of the point of impact.

● Stretching the arm and wrist early (well before the point of impact)
This greatly limits the acceleration of the movement.

Straightening at the elbow and wrist too early lessens the acceleration of the movement.

Bringing the right foot forward too soon leads to early rotation of the upper body, and the absence of transfer of the weight.

Pushing the pelvis back at the point of impact can result in failing to meet the ball at the ideal point of impact.

● Bringing the right foot forwards in the direction of the shot too early
This results in your body turning too early, making it impossible to transfer your weight in the direction of the shot.
● Pushing the pelvis backwards
This leads to your body being stretched too early, preventing the ball from being met at the highest point.
● Poor acceleration of the racket at the point of impact
As a result too little speed and too little spin is imparted to the ball.

A follow-through on the right side of the body makes it virtually impossible to turn the body in the direction of the shot, particularly in the sliced service and straight service.

The follow-through phase
● Racket arm following through on the right side of the body
This prevents your body from turning, particularly in the straight and sliced service.

STROKE TECHNIQUES

Smashing

In which situations and positions is this technique used, and what are its uses and results?
What effects does it have on the ball's behaviour?

Court positions
The smash is most commonly played in the centre part of the court, between the net and about a metre (yard) behind the service line.

Tactical uses
- To smash an easily attainable lob to prevent your opponent from getting to the ball.
- A deep, well-placed lob that can still be returned with a jump smash is to be hit less hard, but well placed, to gain time and to achieve a good starting position from which to continue the attack.
- If the ball cannot be returned with a jump smash, the opponent has the possibility of going into the attack himself.
- To play a backhand smash so that your opponent can't get to it, or is kept at bay; it is played either short, across the court, or long, parallel to the sidelines.
- The jump smash is most commonly played in response to a very good lob from an opponent (2).
- With a very long and high lob, it is played after the ball has bounced (1).
- The backhand smash is a response to a surprise volley

lob or a lob from the centre of the opponent's court played well above the player's backhand side, preventing a normal smash (3).

Effects on the ball's behaviour

- A ball with no spin is generally given considerable speed, and bounces fast, and often high.
- A smash played with spin travels more slowly.

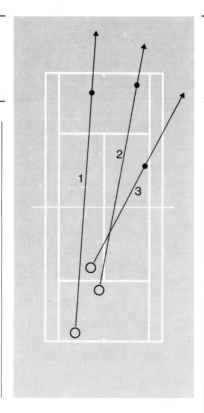

The smash is most commonly hit from the centre part of the court (2, 3), sometimes even after bouncing near the baseline. It should be played so that an opponent is unable to get to it.

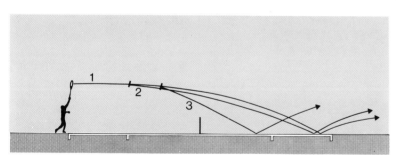

The smash from the baseline (1), after the ball has bounced, is played deep into the opposite court.
The smash from the centre part of the court (2) is played sufficiently hard to prevent an opponent from taking it.
The smash in front of the service line (3) is played across court so that an opponent is unable to get to it.

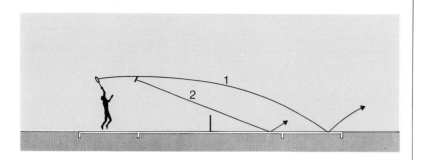

The jump smash in response to a lob that is difficult to get to (1) is played reliably and deep, at average speed.
A smash that is easier to hit in a jump (2) is played at extremely high speed.

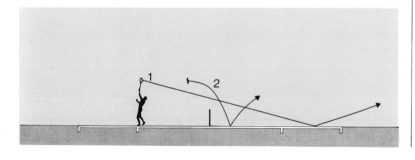

A backhand smash from the service line area (1) should travel as fast as possible.
A backhand smash near the net (2) is played across court.

Follow-through *The racket continues forwards in the direction of the shot, finishing in front of the left half of the body.*

Striking the ball *The racket is accelerated steeply upwards and forwards and the point of impact is in front of the head, with the body, arm and hand fully extended.*

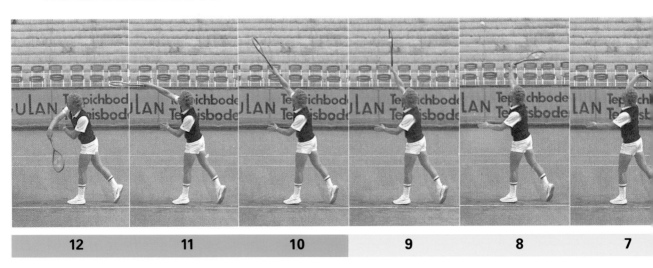

| 12 | 11 | 10 | 9 | 8 | 7 |

FOREHAND SMASH

Basic techniques

This section shows you what you have to do to make the ball do as you intend.

Meeting the ball

● Accelerate the head of your racket sharply upwards and forwards from behind your back to reach the greatest speed at the point of impact (see photographs 6 to 9).
● Your racket should meet the ball a little in front of your head, as in photograph 9, with your racket face pointing slightly forwards at the point of impact to send the ball on the desired trajectory.
● You turn your racket face by twisting your forearm only just before the point of impact, so that the face is perpendicular to the direction of the shot (see photographs 8 and 9).

| 6 | 5 | 4 | 3 | 2 | 1 |

The backswing phase

- You hold your racket in the backhand grip to achieve the best point of impact.
- At the start of the backswing phase, unlike in the service, you take your racket in front of the right side of your body, backwards and upwards, as in photographs 1 and 2. This is mainly for reasons of time.
- Transfer your weight onto your right foot, which is to the rear, as shown in photographs 1 and 2.
- Lean your upper body backward, at the same time turning slightly from the waist into a sideways-on position in relation to the lob's flight path (see photographs 1 to 3).
- To help your balance, your left arm stretches upwards; this also assists the backwards lean of the line of your shoulders (see photograph 2).

The striking phase

- During the hitting action your upper body should turn to assist it, your right shoulder becoming higher than the left.
- Reach with your body towards the point of impact to meet the ball at the greatest height; at the point of impact your body, arm and hand should be fully extended (see photographs 6 to 9). Your weight is on your left foot to enable you to hit the ball at the highest point.

The follow-through phase

- After the point of impact your forearm turns less than in the service, as shown in photographs 9 and 10, and the follow-through ends roughly in front of the left side of your body; the right tilt of the wrist is only slight.
- Your upper body follows the ball and bends further forwards.
- Your left arm moves in front of your body to help keep your balance (see photographs 10 to 12).

Backswing *The weight is shifted onto the back leg and the racket brought backwards and upwards in front of the right side of the body.*

Striking the ball *Pushing off with the right leg, the racket is accelerated through the lowest part of the loop, sharply upwards and*

1   2   3   4   5   6   7

JUMP SMASH

Basic techniques

This section shows you what you have to do to make the ball do as you intend.

Meeting the ball

Accelerate the head of your racket sharply upwards and forwards from behind your back to reach its greatest speed at the point of impact (see photographs 6 to 9).
● Your racket should meet the ball directly above or a little in front of your head, with the racket face upright or tilting slightly forwards at the point of impact, depending on the target, to send the ball on the desired trajectory.
● Bring your racket face perpendicular to the direction of the shot only just before the point of impact, by turning your forearm inwards (see photographs 8 and 9).

The backswing phase

Hold your racket in the backhand grip to achieve the most effective point of impact.
● At the start of the backswing phase, unlike in the service, you bring your racket backwards and upwards in front of the right side of your body, as shown in photographs 1 to 3.
● Shift your body weight onto your right foot, which is placed to the rear.
● Your left arm stretches up to help your balance; this assists the backwards lean of your shoulderline (see photographs 2 and 3)

forwards to the point of impact, which is above or slightly in front of the head.

Follow-through *The right leg continues forwards and upwards until it is in front of the left side of the body and the left foot has landed.*

8   9   10   11   12   13   14

The striking phase

● At the start of the hitting phase, take off from the ground with your right leg (see photographs 4 and 5); this results in a counterbalancing scissor movement of your legs in the air (see photographs 4 to 8).
● Swing your racket through the lowest part of the loop to the point of impact at high speed (see photographs 4 to 7).
● Reach out towards the point of impact by straightening your arm and wrist (photographs 7 to 9).
● Turn your upper body to the front to assist the hitting action, and lean it backwards, with the momentum of your jump (see photographs 6 to 9).
● Hit the ball at the highest point your leap, as in photograph 9.

The follow-through phase

● After the point of impact your forearm rotates later than in the service and the follow-through ends roughly in front of the left side of your body, as shown in photograph 14; the rightwards tilt of your wrist is comparatively slight (see photographs 10 and 11).
● You land on your left foot, with your right leg pointing forwards as a counterbalance and your upper body leaning forwards to a greater or lesser degree, as in photograph 12.
● To help your balance your left arm moves in front of your body (see photographs 10 and 11).

JUMP SMASH

Acceptable variations

The backswing phase

• Many players hold the racket in the centre grip. This grip can, however, cause a certain restriction of movement in your wrist.

• Many players swing back with a pendulum action as in the service: this leads to shortness of time, particularly with fast lobs, and to a late arm swing. In such cases, the pendulum action should be flattened: for many players, however, the pendulum action assists the jump-off action in the jump smash, and gives better co-ordination in the movement overall.

• Depending on how far an opponent's lob is played over your left shoulder, the rotation of the upper body can vary.

• In the jump smash the timing of the jump-off can vary; a relatively early and so higher jump-off allows the hitting action to be delayed slightly and leaves your opponent guessing longer as to how the ball is to be smashed.

The striking phase

• Many players take the loop behind the back as far out as in the service; this can have the disadvantage of the ball being met too late as a result; in addition, in a jump smash, it can lead to co-ordination problems.

• In a deep lob the ball often has to be hit with a pronounced backward lean of the upper body, in which case the fullest force of the body can't be brought to bear; also, more spin is often imparted to this type of smash.

The follow-through phase

• Sometimes, as in the service, the racket is swung left past the body.

• Occasionally it is necessary to hit with the arm only almost without using the body at all, and the upper body remains leaning backwards after impact.

• With a good lob, in which the ball can only be met well behind in spite of jumping, the hitting action is carried out almost exclusively with the arm, and the follow-through ends at chest height; the equalizing scissor action with the right leg must be much more pronounced.

Common mistakes

The backswing phase

• Using the forehand grip
This affects the straightening of your wrist at the point of impact and means you won't be able to hit the ball at the highest point possible.

• Failing to rotate the body
This prevents your body from being used properly, and the stroke becomes unreliable and slow.

• The pendulum action and loop behind the back are as wide as in the service, even where time is short
As a result with fast lobs the path followed by the swing of your racket is too long, and the ball is met too late.

• Failing to move forward with a short lob, to get under the ball
As a result you will meet the ball too far forward, the ball's flight path will be too steep and the ball will generally be hit into the net.

The striking phase

• Low point of impact
The stroke will be executed without shifting your weight forwards and upwards.

• Failing to straighten the racket arm
As a result you will hit the ball with reduced momentum, and not at the highest possible point.

• Moving the racket at an angle to the direction of the shot
This gives the ball considerable spin, and insufficient speed.

A low point of impact in the smash leads to a lack of power behind the shot from a forwards and upwards transfer in the weight.

If the hitting arm is bent it prevents the ball from being met at the ideal point, hinders the body from being used, and reduces the possibility of hitting the ball with any force.

- Meeting the ball to the side, above the right shoulder
This means that you won't hit the ball at the ideal point, and therefore without the maximum force.
- Bringing the upper body forward too early
This means you don't hit the ball at the highest possible point with your body fully stretched.
- Jumping off at the wrong height in the jump smash
This makes hitting the ball at the most effective point impossible.
- Jumping off too early or too late
This upsets the co-ordination of the stroke.

The follow-through phase
- Extremely short follow-through ending in front of the chest
This indicates that too little force was used in hitting the ball.

Landing on the right leg (the jump-off leg) after a jump smash makes it difficult to regain balance and run quickly to a good net position.

- Landing on the right leg after the jump smash
This makes it difficult to regain your balance after hitting the ball.

If the ball is met to the side, above the shoulder, it's impossible to hit the ball with full force and the point of impact is too low.

Backswing *The racket is taken back across the backhand side, backwards and down, and the* *elbow sharply raised, with the body weight transferred onto the back leg before jumping off.* **Striking the ball** *The arm is stretched and the racket accelerated sharply upwards and forwards; the*

1 2 3 4 5 6 7

BACKHAND SMASH

Basic techniques

This section shows you what you have to do to make the ball do as you intend.

Meeting the ball

- Accelerate the head of your racket sharply upwards and forwards (see photographs 7 to 9).
- Your racket face needs to be almost perpendicular to the direction of the shot right at the beginning of the main action (see photograph 9) to ensure a controlled swing of the racket in this position to the point of impact.
- At the point of impact your racket face should be tilted slightly forwards, as shown in photograph 10, to give the ball the required flight path.
- The point of impact should be above and slightly in front of your body (between photographs 9 and 10).

The backswing phase

- Hold your racket in the backhand grip to achieve the ideal point of impact.
- At the start of the backswing phase, bring your racket backwards across your left side, at the same time turning your upper body to the left so that your backhand side points halfway towards the net (see photographs 1 to 4).
- Raise your right elbow so sharply that your racket hangs vertically downwards, as shown in photographs 5 and 6.
- Lean your upper body backwards so that your right shoulder comes up, and the line of your shoulders points sharply upwards (see photographs 4 to 6); this is essential for you to achieve the high point of impact needed in this stroke.
- Transfer your weight onto your left (back) foot, as shown in photographs 1 to 4.

point of impact is above or a little in front of the body with the racket face tipped slightly forwards.

Follow-through *The racket head is tilted downwards, the upper body locked, with the left leg landing first.*

| 8 | 9 | 10 | 11 | 12 | 13 | 14 |

- In the second part of the backswing phase you jump off from your back foot, as shown in photographs 4 and 5, to reach the highest possible point of impact.
- During the backswing phase your left hand should remain at the neck of the racket to the lowest point in the loop to assist and stabilize the backswing action (see photographs 1 to 5).

The striking phase

(The photographs show the stroke played with considerable use of the wrist, as covered in the acceptable variations in the striking phase).
- You reach towards the point of impact initially using your shoulder, then your elbow (photographs 6 to 8) and finally your wrist (photographs 9 and 10). At the point of impact your arm and upper body are fully extended (between photographs 9 and 10).
- The rear of your right shoulder should be half turned towards the net to give the most effective use of the force of your arm.

The follow-through phase

- After the point of impact, given the high speed of the head of the racket on impact, your arm continues to swing in the direction of the shot; your wrist, in particular – partly due to the high speed – is increasingly bent in the direction of the shot, so that the head of your racket tilts sharply downwards (see photographs 10 to 12).
- The back of your right shoulder stays turned towards the net, as shown in photographs 10 to 14.
- Your left arm and right leg counterbalance each other and you land on your left foot.

BACKHAND SMASH

Acceptable variations

The backswing phase
● Many players hold the racket in the centre grip; in this grip, however, it's more difficult to bring your racket face into the ideal position in relation to the ball.
● At the start of the backswing the racket may be taken back past the head, or over the head backwards and upwards in a clear upper arc, or alternatively it may be taken back low.
● Many players don't allow the racket head to drop into the vertical position after the upper arc, and the shortened momentum then has to be made up in the hitting phase by the use of either considerable force or of the wrist.

The striking phase
● Many players don't meet the ball at the highest point, but rather lower and to the right of the right shoulder. They don't stand under the ball; the stroke is then similar to a high backhand volley in which the angle of the stroke is poor.
● Many players in the backhand smash deliberately accelerate the racket to the point of impact with a pronounced use of the wrist; the speed of the stroke is then very fast. An important requirement for this method of hitting, however, is that you have a strong wrist.
● The backhand smash can also be hit from a standing stance.

The follow-through phase
● In the case of a deep lob over the left shoulder, the use of momentum is rather limited, the speed of the stroke is slow and the follow-through is greatly shortened as a result.
● A pronounced use of the wrist in hitting the ball greatly shortens the follow-through: the hitting arm remains pointing almost vertically upwards; the follow-through is limited by the mobility of the wrist.

This is the classic position at the start of the striking phase.

• When the stroke is played from standing the weight is transferred from the left leg onto the right in the direction of the net.
• When the stroke is played from a jump the player generally lands on the same leg as was used to jump off: depending on the point of impact with the ball, however, the player may have to hit the ball in such a way that his back is full on to the net; in this case the legs cross in mid-air so that the player lands on the right leg.

Common mistakes

The backswing phase
• Using the forehand grip
This makes it impossible to meet the ball at the highest point, and the use of your wrist is affected.

• Failing to turn the upper body to the back
This greatly shortens your backswing movement.
• Failing to raise the elbow at the end of the backswing over the right shoulder
This greatly shortens your backswing movement, momentum is reduced, and the ball is often met too low.
• Taking the racket over the left shoulder behind the back
This causes the backswing to be too long, and impairs your control of the movement in the hitting phase.

The striking phase
• Hitting action lacking momentum
If your lower arm fails to hang down loosely enough at the end of the backswing your acceleration of the racket will be limited.
• Failing to stretch the hitting arm and body
As a result the ball will be met with reduced momentum, and not at the highest point.

• Turning the upper body in the direction of the shot
As a result your racket is taken to the right in the hitting phase, impairing your momentum in the direction of the point of impact and the ideal position of the racket face at the point of impact will need to be achieved by rotating your forearm.
• Little or no wrist movement in the main action
As a result your racket won't be accelerated sufficiently, and the ball can't be hit hard enough.

The follow-through phase
• Swinging the entire arm after the point of impact, with the wrist firm
This indicates that the ball was hit with too little momentum.
• Turning the upper body towards the front in the direction of the shot
This indicates that your upper body was turned in the hitting phase.

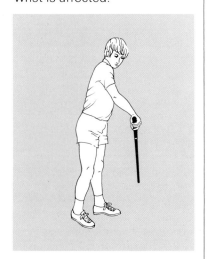

Failing to raise the elbow in the backswing for the backhand smash leads to poor momentum and a low point of impact for the stroke.

If the ball is hit with the arm bent, it's impossible to use sufficient force and the point of impact is too low.

Volleying

In which situations and positions is this technique used and with what intentions and results?
What effects does it have on the ball's behaviour?

Court positions

The volley – both forehand and backhand – is usually played from the service court area (ideally about 2 to 3 metres/ yards from the net).

Tactical uses

• The ball should travel as low as possible towards your opponent's baseline (1), particularly when played from the service court area, keeping him pinned there while allowing you time to take up an advantageous position at the net.
• At the net the ball should be played so as to force your opponent so far out of court that he can't get to the ball at all. (2)
• Balls played at high speed should leave your opponent pressed for time, forcing him to play hasty, uncontrolled shots.
• The use of the volley should leave your opponent no time to take up an ideal position after returning the shot.
• The rally can also be brought to an end by wrong-footing your opponent or playing the ball deep into the opposite corner.

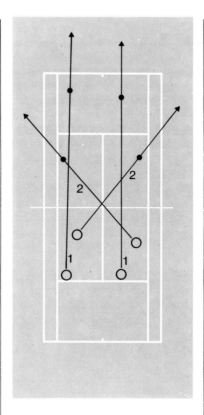

The volley can be played as a connecting volley from the service court area (2) and the rally then be closed out with a winning shot from a good net position (2).

When played from the service line (1) the volley should be played as low and long as possible with backspin.
When played from a good net position (2) the volley should be hit with light backspin and at high speed.

Effects on the ball's behaviour

• The ball speed is relatively high if played from near the net and above net height.
• The ball speed is lower when played further away from the net and below net height.
• In general the ball will have backspin and so fly low.

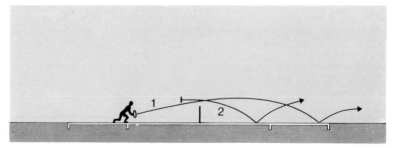

Backswing *The upper body turns with the weight on the left leg, the racket travels a relatively short way back and up and the weight shifts onto the right leg.*

Striking the ball *The racket travels forwards and slightly downwards with a step and shift of weight on to*

1   2   3   4   5

FOREHAND VOLLEY

Basic techniques

This section shows you what you have to do to make the ball do as you intend.

Meeting the ball

- You should move your racket in a forward and slightly downward direction to lend the ball backspin.
- The racket speed should increase towards impact to reach the required tempo for the shot and the ball should be taken as early as possible.
- You should hit the ball to the side of your body and with your wrist firmly locked, meeting the incoming ball with a lot of resistance for a powerful shot; the racket face should be as minimally open as possible and preferably vertical, as in photograph 7.

the left leg; impact is at the side of the body with a strongly braced wrist.

Follow-through *The racket initially continues forwards and down in the direction of the shot and then gently forwards and up.*

| 6 | 7 | 8 | 9 | 10 |

The backswing phase

● At the start of the swing hold your racket in the forehand grip so that the surface of the racket is almost vertical at the point of impact and the ball can be taken in front of the body.

● Twist your upper body back and raise your forearm so that the head of your racket is above the height of the expected point of impact, as in photographs 2 and 3; this allows for a forward and downward stroke action.

● Timing demands that the swing action is considerably shorter than that for ground strokes.

● Shift your body weight onto your right leg, as shown in photograph 2; your left leg doesn't move forward at this stage, allowing you to take a step onto the ball on the shot itself.

The striking phase

● During the forward and downward movement on the shot straighten your arm, as in photographs 4 and 5, with your elbow moving in the direction of the shot; this produces the most effective point of impact.

● During the arm action step into the ball with your left leg (see photographs 4 to 6); this shift of weight forward and down aids the movement on the shot.

● On contact with the ground your left leg should be bent, as in photographs 6 and 7, to aid the forward and downward movement.

● On impact turn your upper body in the direction of the stroke (see photographs 5 to 7) which will help you to take the ball early.

The follow-through phase

● At the start of the follow-through the movement continues forward and down and then ends in a gentle forward and upward direction which returns you smoothly to the starting position (see photographs 8 to 10).

FOREHAND VOLLEY

Acceptable variations

The backswing phase

● Some players hold the racket with the centre grip and if a player uses this grip on the backhand volley, too, there is no need to change grip. The disadvantage is that it lessens the force of the stroke; the point of impact in a near-vertical position of the racket face isn't far enough forward and the wrist is particularly stressed. However, using the centre grip makes it easier to hit the ball with a suitably open racket face on deep volleys.

● On slow balls at a suitable height the backswing action can be more extended so that the arm is almost at full stretch at the end of the movement, the acceleration time is increased and so the ball can be hit harder and deeper into the court.

The striking phase

● On slow balls the movement onto the shot can be more energetic, which can, however, reduce your control over the ball.

● When playing a deep volley, one where the point of impact is below net height, the racket face must be open at impact so that the ball can be played safely over the net.

● On a deep volley the left leg should be in position well before the stroke action; you don't need any support on the stroke action by shifting your body weight as the deep

When playing a deep volley the racket face must be open on impact to allow the ball to fly over the net.

volley isn't played so forcefully and you are better able to keep your balance.

● On very fast balls the stroke action is very short, the ball can almost only be blocked; any more extensive movements would lead to unsure and late shots.

The follow-through phase

● The follow-through, depending on the force of the shot, will be more or less emphatic, making the return to the starting position more or less fluent.

Common mistakes

The backswing phase

● Using the backhand grip
This lessens the force of the shot as the point of impact is too far back and it's hardly possible to have the racket face in a vertical position.

● Very relaxed wrist
This means that the racket head returns too late, making it difficult to play the ball at the right moment and tighten the wrist exactly on impact.

● Very high and wide swing
Taking your forearm too far away from your upper body means that the stroke action doesn't proceed in the intended direction but veers strongly to the left in front of your body.

● Swinging straight back or even backwards and down
This makes the correct up-down movement on the stroke impossible.

A very high and wide swing action on the forehand volley means that the direction of the stroke action is often in front of the body and too little in the direction of the net.

Playing the ball very late on the forehand volley leads to an uncontrolled shot and makes a shift of weight impossible.

The striking phase

● No forward and downward direction of the stroke action
This leads to a lack of certainty and control.

● Excessive exaggeration of the downwards movement
This does produce backspin but the ball can't be played deep into the court and doesn't have much speed.

● Not hitting sufficiently in the direction of the shot
This makes it difficult to control the shot.

● Very late impact on the ball
In this case shifting your weight becomes impossible.

● No tensing of the wrist on hitting the ball
This leads to a significant reduction in your accuracy and control in the volley.

● Absence or lateness of weight shifting
This means that the movement is made with the arm only, leading to a lack of co-ordination in the movement and of ball control.

The follow-through phase

● Very early start to the movement upwards in the follow-through
This leads to a significant reduction in your ball control on the volley.

Follow-through *The racket initially continues forwards and down in the direction of the shot and then turns gently forwards and up.*

Striking the ball *The racket moves forwards and slightly downwards; the racket arm straightens and the weight shifts onto the right leg.*

10   9   8   7

BACKHAND VOLLEY

Basic techniques

This section shows you what you have to do to make the ball do as you intend.

Meeting the ball

- You should move your racket in a forward and slightly downward direction to give the ball backspin.
- Your racket speed should increase towards impact to reach the required tempo for the shot and so that you take the ball as early as possible.
- You should hit the ball in front and to the side of your body with your wrist firmly locked so that the approaching ball meets with a lot of resistance, making for a powerful stroke; your racket face should be almost vertical (see photograph 7).

The backswing phase

- At the start of the swing hold your racket in the backhand grip so that the racket face will be almost vertical at the point of impact and the ball can be taken in front of your body.
- Pivot your upper body so far back that the line of your shoulders is parallel to the direction of the shot. Raise your forearm slightly, as shown in photographs 2 and 3, to prepare for the forward and downward stroke action.
- Timing means that your backswing is considerably shorter than for ground strokes.
- During the backswing keep your left hand at the neck of your racket to help the backward twist of your upper body (see photograph 3).

Impact is to the side and in front of the body with the wrist firmly braced.

Backswing *The upper body twists sharply with the weight firmly on the left leg and the racket is pulled a*

relatively short distance backwards and up supported by the left hand.

| 6 | 5 | 4 | 3 | 2 | 1 |

• Shift your body weight onto your left leg (photograph 2); your right leg doesn't move forward at this stage (see photographs 2 and 3) allowing you to take a step onto the ball on the shot itself.

The striking phase

• Straighten your arm fully, as shown in photographs 4 to 6, to produce the required racket acceleration and to make sure you take the ball early.
• As you are straightening your arm, shift your weight onto your right foot (see photographs 3 to 7).
• Bend your right leg on contact with the ground, as in photographs 4 to 7, to further your forward and downward movement.
• Keep the line of your shoulders parallel to the direction of the shot (see photograph 7) for the most effective play on the ball.
• Move your left arm slightly behind you to maintain your balance and your sideways-on stroke position (see photographs 8 and 9).

The follow-through phase

• At the start of the follow-through the movement continues forwards and down in the direction of the shot and then ends in a gentle forward and upward movement (photographs 8 to 10) returning you smoothly to the starting position.

107

BACKHAND VOLLEY

Acceptable variations

The backswing phase

● When playing the backhand volley some players hold the racket with the centre grip, which is suitable for deep volleys. For balls taken above net height, however, the racket face should be very open and needs to be corrected by bending the wrist which is then placed under considerable stress, limiting the power behind the shot.

The striking phase

● On slow balls the movement onto the shot can be more energetic, speeding up the ball without any effort.
● When playing a low volley, one where the point of impact is below net height, the racket face must be open on impact so that the ball can be played safely over the net.
● On a deep volley the right leg should be in position well before the stroke action; as the deep volley isn't generally played so forcefully you don't need the support on the stroke action resulting from shifting your body weight.
● On very fast balls the stroke action is very short so that the ball can be taken on time.

The follow-through phase

● The extent of the follow-through varies in relation to the force of the stroke; in extreme circumstances it can be dispensed with entirely; your return to the starting position will be correspondingly fluent.

A backhand volley, which can be played across the opponent's forehand side as, for example, a tactical variant in a doubles match.

Common mistakes

The backswing phase

- Using the forehand grip
This lessens the power of the shot and makes the point of impact too far back.
- No support for the swing action from the left hand
This often leads to your upper body not being turned sufficiently or even at all, leaving the point of impact too near to the side of the body; the stroke action is then more of a jerk than a swing.
- Swinging straight back or even backwards and down
This makes the correct up-down movement on the stroke impossible.

The striking phase

- No forwards and downwards direction of the stroke action
This leads to a lack of accuracy and control.
- Excessive exaggeration of the downwards movement
This does produce backspin but the ball can't be played deep into the court and doesn't acquire much speed.
- Not hittng sufficiently in the direction of the shot
This makes it difficult to control the shot.
- Failing to straighten the racket arm
This makes the point of impact too near your side and the movement veers to the right and not in the desired forwards direction, producing sidespin on the ball.
- Rotating the upper body during the stroke action

A bent arm at the point of impact in the backhand volley means that the ball isn't played at the ideal distance from the body. It often makes the stroke action veer off to the right instead of forwards in the direction of the net.

Early rotation of the upper body on the backhand volley leads to an inexact and uncontrolled shot on the ball.

This makes an exact shot impossible.
- Very late impact on the ball
This makes shifting your weight impossible.
- No tensing of the wrist on hitting the ball
This leads to a significant reduction of your accuracy and control in the volley.
- Absence of, or too early weight shift
This means that the movement is made with your arm only, leading to a lack of co-ordination in your movement and ball control.

The follow-through phase

- Very early start to the upward follow-through
This leads to a significant reduction of your control over the ball.

STROKE TECHNIQUES

Drop shots

In which situations and positions is this technique used and what are its uses and outcomes?
What effects does it have on the ball's behaviour?

Court positions
● Drop shots – forehand and backhand – are usually played from between the baseline and service line.
● The stop volley is played from near the net, especially when taken at or below net height.

Tactical uses
● To play the ball in such a way that it bounces just beyond the net.
● The ball should bounce neither very far nor very high so that your opponent is unable to reach it or is forced to play it from very low (shortly before its second bounce).
● It is possible to play a winning shot if your opponent is very far off the ball or moving in the opposite direction to it.
● A drop shot is used to tempt a baseline player forward to the net.
● A drop shot forces an opponent to run in and so may cause him to tire more easily.
● If your opponent plays a drop shot it is possible to play a winning shot by playing a 'counter-drop' or at least to gain a useful position.

The stop volley is often hit across court. It is played below net height and travels with backspin.

● Sometimes a stop volley is useful when returning low balls or topspin passing shots as it can be difficult to volley a low ball deep into the court.

Effects on the ball's behaviour
● The ball has a great deal of backspin.
● The curve of the ball's flight should dip sharply immediately beyond the net.
● The ball bounces slowly and not very high.

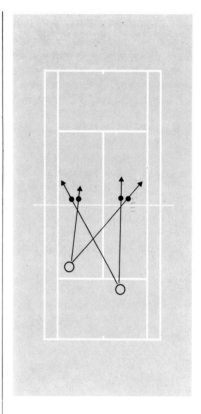

The drop shot is usually played from between the service line and baseline, the stop volley from right up at the net. It is used to make a winning shot or to force an opponent to run.

The drop shot travels with backspin, should dip sharply into the opponent's court and not bounce too far into it.

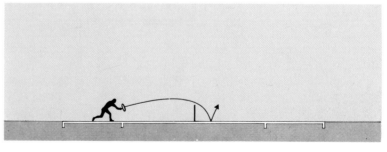

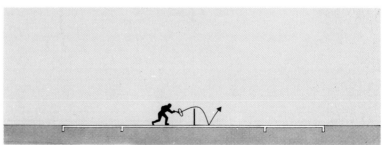

Backswing *The upper body is turned backwards, the racket is taken slightly back and raised above* *the point of impact and the left leg moves forwards in the direction of the shot.* **Striking the ball** *The racket moves forwards and down, the left leg bends, the upper body turns in the*

| 1 | 2 | 3 | 4 | 5 |

DROP SHOT

Basic techniques

This section shows you what you have to do to make the ball do as you intend.

Meeting the ball

- You bring your racket forwards and downwards from slightly above and behind your head, as shown in photographs 5 to 7, to produce backspin.
- Move your racket relatively slowly towards impact either to stop a fast incoming ball or to avoid imparting too much speed to a slow ball.
- The point of impact (see photograph 7) should be at waist height, with your wrist tensed and your racket almost vertical to produce the relatively low curve you want.

direction of the shot, with the point of impact in front of the body at hip level.

Follow-through *The forearm turns and there is a short forward and upward follow-through.*

| 6 | 7 | 8 | 9 | 10 |

The backswing phase

● For a forehand drop use the forehand grip, for a backhand drop use the backhand grip.
● Make your backswing action relatively short to reduce the power of the stroke on impact.
● Twist your upper body back to support the swing action (see photographs 1 to 3); in the case of a backhand drop your left hand also remains at the neck of the racket.
● Your left leg (in the forehand drop shot, the right for the backhand), which takes your weight during the stroke action and follow-through, steps forward and to the side, as in photographs 3 and 4. To maintain good balance your feet should be farther apart than the width of your body.

The striking phase

● Keep the leg nearer the net bent during the stroke action (see photographs 5 to 7) to support the forward and downward movement; this also helps your co-ordination between the arm movement and the shift of weight.
● For the forehand drop shot turn your upper body slightly through the direction of the shot, as in photographs 6 and 7; for the backhand drop shot maintain your sideways-on position for the most effective stroke and ball control.
● Straighten your arm on the shot, more fully for the backhand than for the forehand drop shot (see photograph 7).

The follow-through phase

● A short forward and upward follow-through should begin immediately the ball is hit (see photographs 8 to 10); this indicates that the speed and spin were well-judged to produce an accurately placed drop shot.
● Turn your forearm until your racket face is almost parallel to the ground, as shown in photographs 9 and 10; this helps keep the follow-through action ideally compact.
● Straighten your leg nearest the net; this supports the upwards movement on the follow-through and helps co-ordinate your arm and body movement (see photograph 10).

DROP SHOT

Acceptable variations

The backswing phase
● When playing a drop shot (on both the forehand and backhand) some players use the centre grip; this makes the desired opening of the racket face after impact easier.
● A relatively wide swing action, similar to that for a slice, disguises the drop shot to your opponent.
● The racket face can, particularly in the case of the forehand drop shot, be slightly closed at the end of the backswing action; as a rule this makes it easier to achieve

A drop shot without a forward and upward follow-through ('chop'); the racket face is not opened any further after impact.

the correct racket face position on impact and makes the transition to the follow-through correspondingly short and fluent.

The striking phase
● In the case of relatively fast incoming balls the forward movement can be dispensed with almost entirely: the ball is simply stopped and given plenty of backspin.
● On impact there is an occasional slackening of the wrist; the speed of the incoming ball is reduced accordingly and receives less backspin. The danger here lies in the difficulty of controlling the ball.
● The position of the racket face on impact can be more or less open; it's open if the point of impact is low and if the ball is played on the descent after the bounce; this allows the ball to be played safely over the net.

● If, in competitive play, you want to deceive your opponent about the shot, then it is not only the swing action but also the beginning of the stroke action that must look like a slice: the principal drop shot action (reduced racket speed on impact) is only applied late.

The follow-through phase
● The height and width of the follow-through action will vary according to the speed of the shot and scale of the racket action.
● With no upward follow-through, the action continues forward and down in the direction of the shot; the racket face is not opened any further, the stroke action is suddenly braked and there is a lack of fluidity in the movement and a weak fade-out to the action. However, there is good control of the racket face position.

Common mistakes

The backswing phase

● Little or no twist of the upper body
This leaves you with no basis for the control of a sensitive stroke action.
● Swing action direction straight back
This makes any forward and downward directed stroke action impossible. Both the height and distance of the ball are difficult to control.
● Very late follow-through
This makes it impossible to employ the smooth stroke action required, and badly impairs your control over the ball.

The striking phase

● Forearm turned and racket face opened widely before hitting the ball
Although this does produce the desired backspin on the ball it makes it fly off very high.
● Stoke action too energetic
This makes control of the ball speed and distance of shot almost impossible.
● No bending of the knee nearer to the net
This produces a lack of co-ordination in the action of your body as a whole. The stroke action is produced by your arm alone and your control of the shot is impaired.
● Straightening the leading leg very early
This causes your weight to be shifted upwards and often backwards, the co-ordination of the action is disturbed and the flight of the ball is too short and very high.
● Wrist very relaxed on impact
Although this does slow down the incoming ball it also prevents you from controlling the spin and trajectory.

The follow-through phase

● Late start to the follow-through
This indicates that your racket speed at impact was too high and so the incoming ball couldn't be sufficiently blocked, making it impossible to control the spin and length of the trajectory.

Although having a wide open racket face before the ball is struck produces strong backspin it also causes the ball to fly off too high.

Backswing *The upper body twists and there is a short, upward movement of the racket.*

Striking the ball *The racket moves briefly forward and downward and the point of impact is well in front of*

the body with more or less open racket face and a relaxed forearm and wrist.

1   2   3   4

STOP VOLLEY

Basic techniques

This section shows you what you have to do to make the ball do as you intend.

Meeting the ball

• Your racket action should be short and directed steeply downwards and forwards to produce backspin, as shown in photographs 2 and 3.
• Your racket moves at very low speed to stop the incoming ball appropriately.
• The point of impact should be well in front of your body, as in photograph 3; your racket face should be more or less open on impact; in a longline stop volley your wrist is less tensed than on a cross-court stop volley.

The backswing phase

• The forehand stop volley is made using the forehand grip, the backhand stop volley with the backhand grip.
• Turn your upper body slightly to the rear, keeping the upward and backward swing action of your arm very short as the shot requires very little energy (see photographs 1 and 2).

Follow-through *The racket head dips downwards and back in a short forward and upward follow-through.*

| 5 | 6 | 7 | 8 |

The striking phase

● Bend your leading leg during the stroke action (see photographs 2 and 3) to achieve an ideal point of impact; your arm action is well co-ordinated with a shift of weight.
● Your arm shouldn't be fully extended at impact (see photograph 3), as for the slice and volley, so the incoming ball can be more sensitively blocked. The blocking action is produced by relaxing your forearm and wrist.
● During the stroke action keep your upper body relatively still; this can increase the accuracy of the shot.

The follow-through phase

● The combination of the deeply angled forward and downward racket movement in the main action with the relaxation of your forearm and wrist results in your racket head tipping backwards and down after impact (see photographs 4 and 5). This is especially true of the forehand stop volley; in the backhand stop volley your racket is tipped by twisting your forearm and bending your elbow.
● The follow-through action is a very short forward and upward movement.

STOP VOLLEY

Acceptable variations

The backswing phase

● The already short swing action can be dispensed with entirely; i.e. the racket is moved immediately forwards to the point of impact so the ball can be played early and with appropriately little force.

The striking phase

● The deeper stop volley can also be played with a braced wrist in which case the necessary relaxation on the shot is in the forearm only. Controlling the distance on the stop volley, however, is more difficult in this case.
● Some players strike the ball with their arm well bent, making the distance to the point of impact shorter which, in that case, can lead to better ball control.
● The forward and downward action with the racket can be omitted: the racket is brought to the expected point of impact with the racket face at the appropriate angle, the incoming ball ricochets off the strings and the wrist is bent back according to the force of the incoming ball. This form of stop volley demands a great deal of feel for the ball.
● The racket face can be positioned at an angle to the flight of the incoming ball: with the wrist locked on impact the ball rebounds at an acute angle to the net; the disadvantage of a longer flight is compensated for by the ball's new direction (away from the opponent).

The follow-through phase

● The extent of the follow-through depends on if and to what degree the racket is moved forward and down on impact and whether the wrist and forearm are relaxed.

Common mistakes

The backswing phase

● Very long and rapid stroke action
This makes the shot too powerful and the ball travels too far.
● Arm bent too much when striking the ball
This limits your feel for the ball.
● Racket face not appropriately angled to the path of the incoming ball when blocking
This makes the stop volley either too long if the angle isn't acute enough, or the ball may land in your own court if the angle is too acute.
● Late impact
This severely diminishes your control over the ball.
● Poor co-ordination of the arm action and shift of weight
This also lessens your ball control.

The follow-through phase

● Very obvious and high follow-through action
This indicates that the speed of your stroke action was too great and the flight of the ball too high.

Half volleying

In which situations and positions and with what intentions and results is this technique used?
What are the effects on the ball's behaviour?

Court positions
● The half volley, both forehand and backhand, is most often played from the service line area.
● The half volley is used if the player is too close to the bounce to play a ground stroke but too far to play a volley; this means the half volley can be played from all other positions.

Tactical uses
● To hit the ball as close to your opponent's baseline as possible to allow you to take up an advantageous position at the net and keep your opponent at the baseline.
● By playing the half volley between the service line and baseline you avoid being pushed back or even so far out of position that you would have to play the stroke on the retreat.
● In situations where it's difficult to judge the direction and speed of the bounce (topspin, sidespin, wind, uneven surface) it's possible to return the ball fairly safely using the half volley.
● The half volley can speed up the game; your opponent is put under pressure as the ball is returned quickly to his side.

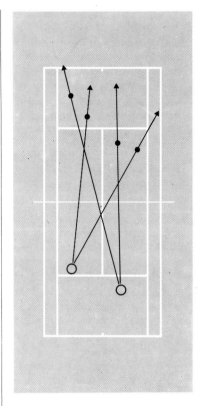

The half volley is usually played from the service line area; it is used to put an opponent under pressure and when a player is near the bounce but can't play the volley.

Effects on the ball's behaviour
● The ball travels at medium speed.
● It should travel low over the net.
● It should bounce low.

The half volley travels low over the net at medium speed.

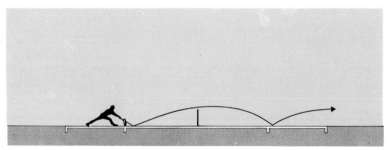

Backswing *The upper body twists, the racket moves back in a very slight upward arc and the right leg bends deeply.*

Striking the ball *The racket is lowered, the left leg positioned well forward in the direction of the shot (this may require sliding) the weight*

1   2   3   4   5   6

HALF VOLLEY

Basic techniques

This section shows you what you have to do to make the ball do as you intend.

● Initially you should move your racket almost parallel to the ground, as shown in photographs 5 to 8, so you can hit the ball immediately off the bounce.
● Accelerate the racket into the shot.
● You should hit the ball level with your leading foot with your wrist locked (see photograph 8), to control the ball and hit it as powerfully as possible.
● The position of your racket face will depend on the speed of both the incoming ball and your racket as well as the distance from the net.

is shifted onto the left leg, the racket swings almost parallel to the ground and the ball is hit at the height of the left foot.

Follow-through *The racket continues forwards and up.*

| 7 | 8 | 9 | 10 | 11 | 12 |

The backswing phase

● Use the forehand racket grip for the forehand half volley and the backhand grip for the backhand half volley.
● Turn your upper body to support the swing action, as shown in photographs 1 to 3.
● Your backswing action should be a very slight upward arc to the rear to enable you to swing your racket back through almost parallel to the ground.
● Your right leg bends deeply on the forehand half volley, your left one on the backhand (see photographs 3 and 4) to support the deep dip of the racket head to the height of the coming point of impact.

The striking phase

● Plant your leading leg well forward in the direction of the shot to stabilize yourself in this deep position (see photographs 5 to 8).
● Shift your weight emphatically onto your forward leg during the stroke action, keeping your centre of gravity low by keeping your leading leg well bent (see photographs 5 to 8); this shift of weight enables you to swing your racket deep and parallel to the ground to an early point of impact.

The follow-through phase

● The follow-through movement is forwards and up, with your leading leg more or less bent (see photographs 9 to 12).

HALF VOLLEY

A generous backswing action on the half volley allows the ball to be struck with great force; this is only possible if there's enough time

The follow-through on a hard hit half volley rises steeply forwards and up.

Acceptable variations

The backswing phase
● The racket can be held with the centre grip; on the backhand half volley this can hinder you from attaining the racket face position needed for early impact.
● The swing action can be relatively generous if there is enough time and the ball is to be played very energetically from the baseline area, from the service line area or near the net with heavy topspin.
● If the half volley is played attackingly while moving forward the twist of the upper body to support the follow-through can be dispensed with.
● The backswing action can also be backwards and downwards to allow you to reach the height of the coming point of impact quickly.

The striking phase
● Depending on circumstances, the point of impact can be in the area between the middle of the body and the foot nearer the net or even be well ahead of the foot; the length of the step is more or less marked accordingly.
● The length of the stroke action varies according to where the shot played; if it's well in front of the body the action is long, if the point of impact comes later then it tends to be short.
● The direction of the stroke action can be more or less steeply forwards and up

depending on the distance the half volley is played from the net; the closer the position to the net the steeper the direction.

• In the case of a topspin half volley the main action is directed particularly steeply forwards and up.

• The length of the step on the forward leg and with it the shift of weight depend on the distance to the point of impact.

The follow-through phase

• If the shot is hit at high speed the follow-through is markedly forwards and upwards.

• If the half volley is played from near the net or with topspin the follow-through is steeply forwards and up in the corresponding direction of the stroke action.

Common mistakes

The backswing phase

• Back leg bent very late or not at all
This makes the movement to the deep point of impact impossible.

• Very high swing action
This makes it very difficult to move your racket to the right height in time.

The striking phase

• Very little bending at the knee
This means your racket head

has to be dipped to reach the ball just above the ground; your shift of weight and power behind the shot are seriously inhibited.

• Very early straightening of the forward leg from the deep position
If you rise before hitting the ball, you won't be able to take it low enough, which will seriously lessen your control of it.

The follow-through phase

• Low follow-through off a half volley at net height
This indicates that your racket action was too low; the ball will travel too low and land in the net.

If the legs are straightened during the hitting phase the racket hangs too low, limiting the force of the shot.

Straightening the legs very early leads to a severe reduction of ball control and rather a high point of impact.

VARIATIONS IN STROKE TECHNIQUES

Playing backwards between the legs.

Playing backwards to the side of the body.

Playing backwards over the left shoulder.

The shots described so far are strokes that arise more or less frequently and which are appropriate for particular situations. In tennis, however, conditions are seldom ideal: there are enormous differences in the circumstances you can be faced with. You often can't play the classic version of a stroke, but according to the particular situation you find yourself in, will need to improvise shots such as those in the series of photographs above.

We won't cover the execution of these variations in technique in detail, but briefly describe the circumstances in which the need for them might arise.

Emergency shots
For example, it often happens that a player at the net is lobbed and can't play a smash. He has to turn around and try to chase the lob. If he is not quick enough to take up a position for one of the more conventional strokes he can play the ball on the run with his back to the net; in this

124

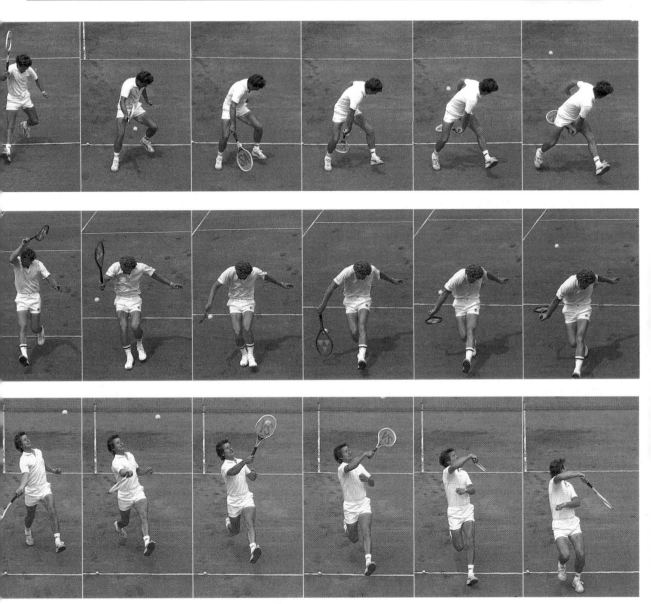

situation the ball will travel in
the opposite direction and,
depending on the position of
the racket face, more or less
high over the net. The stroke
action can be
- between the legs,
- to the right of the body,
- over the left shoulder.

FOOTWORK

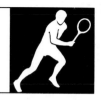

Vital groundwork

Although the most conspicuous feature of tennis playing is the use of the racket, tennis is also very much a running sport: there is no tennis stroke that isn't influenced by footwork.

Moving into position for a shot from a position of readiness, having assessed the speed and direction of an approaching ball, is the first and basic element of a successful stroke.

An analysis of world-class players clearly demonstrates that sound footwork is fundamental to their success.

Individual step and running techniques constantly change in the course of a game; fluent and fast transitions between them depend on the circumstances and the player's skill, athleticism and reaction.

Good and experienced players use combinations of movements instinctively, without thinking about them. Experience also teaches how quickly you should start to run, when to slow down, at what distance to make the penultimate step before a shot, that you shouldn't take up a fixed position on the shot too early or you'll find it difficult to correct the distance to the point of impact later, and that you must always be on the move.

The tips given in this chapter should be treated flexibly as the variety of options in footwork is particularly great.

A player who has been driven way off the court tries to cover ground quickly.

REACHING AN IDEAL HITTING POSITION

For you to make the most effective swing with your racket you need to be the ideal distance from the ball for a particular stroke, which can only be achieved by successful footwork. You may need to do some fine tuning with your footwork to reach the precise position in relation to the ball for the stroke action, depending on your starting position.

You should preferably reach a nearly ideal position on your penultimate step, i.e. on a step with your right leg for a forehand stroke and with one on your left foot for a backhand shot. The better adjusted your penultimate step the more exact your final one will be. Ultimately, however, you can make a final correction in the course of the hitting phase by adjustments of your ankle, knee and hip joints.

The precision of your footwork in bringing you the correct distance from the ball immediately before and during the shot is particularly important on hard, artificial, carpet or grass courts where sliding is almost impossible.

Getting into the best position for a stroke should be achieved by series of movements that are suitable for the circumstances, economical and well-timed.

Economical in this case means energy-saving, taking into account the individual player's temperament.

Timing

Well-timed means neither starting too late, nor getting to the final position for the stroke too early, allowing the series of movements to flow smoothly into one another.

Speed

In a sprint on court a tennis player has a maximum of 14 metres (45 ½ feet) to run. Most sprints are between 2.5 and 6 metres, with an average of 4 metres (8 to 20 feet, average 13 feet). This means that take-off power (at the start) and speed of power (in a short sprint) are all-important in tennis.

Adaptability

According to the constantly changing state of play during a game you will need adaptability to run not only straight, but often in different curves, and sideways and backwards, which calls for a high degree of agility and co-ordination.

The high speed at which tennis is played, and the constantly changing demands imposed by quickly changing states of play, call for very varied footwork and the ability to change course and speed very fast. It involves running not only straight, but also often in curves. It is likely that in any game you will have to run forwards, forwards at an angle, or backwards at an angle.

You may need, for example, to use sidesteps, cross-over steps, or changing steps, which we describe later and strokes such as smashes and volleys may also have to be played from a jump.

In addition you will often be forced to hit the ball from the unorthodox, or wrong foot, from a leaning position, with your knees bent low and at very high speed.

These very demanding situations, in particular, require good footwork, which will often be your only way out of a difficulty.

It is also important to move easily and flexibly on the court, never to stand still with both feet planted on the ground, but to remain active and poised at all times, ready to move in any direction at any time.

You will need to practise your stepping, running and other items of footwork until they are second nature to you, and you can co-ordinate and improvise in the heat of a game without having to think about it.

Co-ordination

The movement in delivering a stroke begins from the ground and works upwards: it is a chain reaction of the individual parts of your body involved in the stroke. This generally requires a stable foot position suitable for the particular type of stroke. As the first link in the chain reaction the correct co-ordination of the movement depends on it.

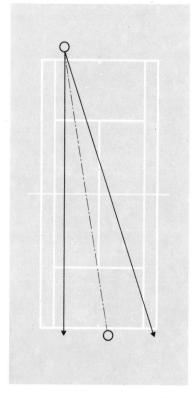

The ideal starting position is half way between the possible limits within which an opponent can play a good shot.

Starting positions

The right starting position is essential for a good prompt start in any direction.
Your body should be relaxed,

Starting position, awaiting a service.

with your feet approximately shoulders' width apart, your knees slightly bent and your upper body also leaning slightly forward. Your body weight will be mainly on the balls of your feet.

You should adopt this position in normal circumstances to wait for the ball about 1 to 1.5 metres (3 or 4 feet) behind the baseline, at the mid-line of the limits within which your opponent will be playing his shot.

Take-off and running

From the starting position you should always start towards the intended stroke with the leg nearer the side of the stroke. Ideally the first step

The first step towards the position for the stroke is made with the leg nearer the side of the stroke.

should be forwards and at an angle towards the oncoming ball: if forced, however, you can take this step to the side or back.

The number of steps depends on the distance from the point of impact, of course. Steps should be small.

Different types of footwork for this phase include
● Triple steps in rapid sequence, on the spot, on the balls of the feet, and jumping on the spot on both legs; these movements tend to be used particularly when waiting for an opponent's shot.
● Side steps: these should be used primarily to cover short distances into position to play the shot, and to resume a

Movement into position for the stroke is by sidestepping so that the body is always facing the net, and wrong-footing is avoided.

good starting position after playing the shot.

● Cross-over steps: these are customarily used as a transition into other types of running, and to assist the movement of your weight in the hitting action.

● Adjustment steps: these are used to make the final correction to the distance before taking up your position for a stroke.

● The sprint, which is similar to the sprint in athletics, is used primarily to cover long distances quickly.

The backwards cross-over step (the tango step) is normally used for an attacking ball with a backhand slice.

When the upper part of the player's body is already leaning towards the net, he runs forward using a cross-over step.

TAKING UP YOUR HITTING POSITION

The last step but one before a stroke should be with your right foot in a forehand stroke and your left foot for a backhand shot.

The last step, taken with your left foot in the forehand and your right foot in the backhand, should as far as possible be in the intended direction of the shot. This will help you to co-ordinate the stroke action with the transfer of your weight and the follow-through.

The two main hitting positions are sideways-on and open. In the backhand the sideways-on position is generally adopted. In the forehand, both positions may be used. The sideways-on position is adopted primarily for ground strokes, and the open position mainly for topspin strokes.

You should always try to play your shots from a firm-footed position, as this increases the precision and reliability of your stroke. Attacking strokes and strokes that have to be hit with considerable body speed are generally run out, with your front foot either still in the air during the hitting action, or landing at the start of the hitting action, and crossing over the back foot (tango step in the sliced backhand).

During the hitting action your body weight is generally shifted from the back foot to the front. This transfer of weight should be completed before the point of impact, even earlier in the backhand than in the forehand. The main

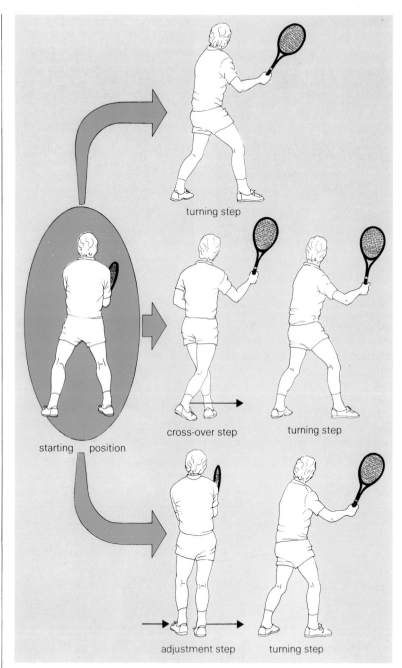

turning step

starting position

cross-over step   turning step

adjustment step   turning step

reason for this is to increase the power behind the stroke from the leg nearer the hitting arm.

This leading leg is also referred to as the bracing leg. For right-handers it is always

The sideways movement begins with either a turning step, a cross-over step or an adjustment step.

the right leg, and for left-handers always the left leg. It is only by taking your weight

Sideways-on hitting position for a forehand drive.

Open hitting position for a topspin forehand drive.

onto your leading leg in this way that you can co-ordinate ideally with all the other parts of your body involved in the stroke and so further the momentum of the shot.

Sideways-on hitting position for a backhand drive.

Footwork Techniques

The following section explains how the basics of footwork can be applied in the main situations encountered in a game of tennis. This is based on the following approach:

● During a game you will find yourself in a number of different positions on court: for example, at the baseline, at the service line area, or in the net area.

● Except in the case of your own servce, you have to react to the balls hit by your opponent and to try to hit them back in the most favourable hitting position possible.

● If possible you return the ball in such a way in terms of speed, placement and spin that you put your opponent at bay.

For different strokes and circumstances footwork is described in terms of

● Starting positions in various places for taking off in different directions.

● Taking off and running from different starting positions to the hitting position:
– to the side
– at an angle or straight forwards
– at an angle or straight backwards.

● Footwork during the hitting action
– in a stationary hitting position
– when hitting in motion
– when hitting from a jump

● Footwork after a stroke and taking up the starting position for the next stroke in a favourable location in the court.

Starting positions

Service

For the service the starting position is just behind the baseline, and generally up to 1 metre (yard) to the right or left of the centre mark in a singles game. Most players stand closer to the centre mark when serving from the right than when serving from the left. In doubles games the distance is greater in both directions.

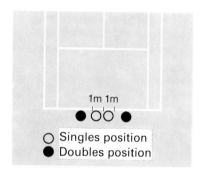

Positions taken up for the service vary between individuals, and are also governed by such factors as the type of service.

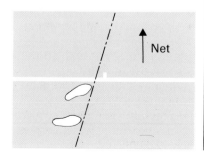

In the classic starting position an imaginary line between the toes points in the intended direction of the shot.

The classic foot position is with the left foot pointing in the direction of the right-hand post of the net, the right foot parallel to the baseline, the feet shoulders' width apart and an imaginary line between the front of the feet pointing in the direction of the shot.

This is often varied by players, whose individual style departs from it particularly in the positioning (direction) of the feet, the distance between them, whether close together or wide apart, and the pace. The distance between the feet also depends on the player's size and the intended stroke: a slice or twist service, for instance, can also influence foot positioning.

Beginning the service with the feet wide apart (over hips' width apart).

Beginning the service with the feet close together.

Definite walking position in the service, with the feet not far apart.

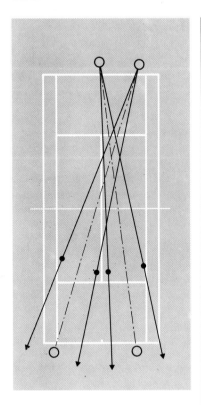

The starting position for the return of service varies in relation to the server's position.

Return of service

Before adopting the starting position for the return of service you should move either alternately from side to side or backwards and forwards, or rise up and down on the balls of your feet. These movements keep you in readiness to react.

For the return of service you should stand half way between the two outside limits of a good service by your opponent. Whether you stand in front of, on or behind the baseline depends on the quality of your opponent's service and your own ability and intentions.

It is advisable to stand in such a way that you will

always be able to hit the return in a forward movement of the body.

A starting position well behind the baseline has the disadvantage that the angle to be covered, and hence the distance from the point of impact, is considerable. You can only afford to adopt a starting position in front of the baseline if you have good reactions, good anticipation (the ability to foresee a situation), and speed of action.

To receive an opponent's second service you should generally stand a little further forward, as this service is not as a rule played as fast as the first, and is easier to attack.

Baseline, service line and net strokes

In baseline, service line and net play your starting position

Correct starting position to await a service.

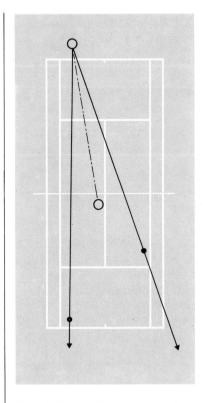

The starting position in net play lies on the mid-line between the outside limits to which any good return shot might be played by an opponent.

should be one where you are standing mid-way between the outside limits to which any good return shot might be played by your opponent. The geometric centre of the court isn't therefore always the ideal position to wait for your opponent's ball.

The starting position in baseline play is about a metre (yard) behind the baseline and in net play about 2 to 3 metres (6 to 10 feet) from the net.

The correct stance in the starting position is with your feet over hips' width apart, your ankles and knees slightly bent and your upper body leaning forwards to a greater or lesser extent. This stance is adopted only very briefly.

At the moment when an opponent's racket meets the ball players frequently spring into a slight stride position from which they then immediately take off, by pushing off from the balls of their feet, into the hitting position. This spring into the stride position allows an equally good take-off in any direction. The timing is crucial: the spring must be neither too early nor too late if you are to reach the ideal hitting position at the right time.

At the precise moment when the opponent hits the ball, the player springs into the stride position.

Take-off and running

The footwork in take-off and running begins immediately after the starting position has been adopted, and ends with the penultimate step before the stroke is played from the hitting position, or with the last step where the stroke is played from an open position.

SIDEWAYS TAKE-OFF AND RUN

Return of service
Because of the speed of the approaching ball the sideways movement into the hitting position to return an opponent's first service usually consists of just one step. This step, with your leg nearer the point of impact, takes the form of a short turning step.

You can avoid relatively slow services either coming directly at the body or that you want to run around (returning with the forehand rather than the backhand) with an adjustment step to the side.

Baseline strokes
In baseline play your distance from the hitting position may be short or long. Shorter distances can be covered with a turning step (turning your upper body at the same time), a cross-over step (a forwards movement), an adjusting step

or sidesteps followed by a turning step (see illustration on page 131).

To cover longer distances you should start with a turning step, a sidestep or a cross-over step, and then sprint into the hitting position. To cover longer distances you should accelerate quickly at first by taking short steps on the balls of your feet. After three to five steps you should start making longer, more flat-footed steps. You should slow your speed down again before reaching the hitting position to enable you to adopt the best hitting position with a good balance.

Service line and net strokes
When you play an opponent's ball at the service line or net, you generally have to play a volley. As in the return of service, there is usually only time for your sideways movement to be a single short turning step with the leg nearer the point of impact. This allows you to take a further step with your other leg in the direction of the point of impact, in order to hit the ball.

A longer lunge step to the side would make you lose your balance, be too much face-on, and prevent you from taking any further step. As a result your reach would be much less than with the turning step (see page 136).

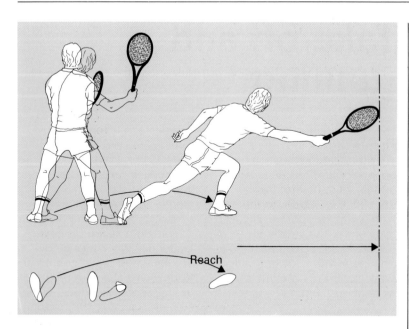

Above: *A turning step to the right and a step with the left leg in the direction of the point of impact gives the maximum reach.*

Below: *A straightforward lunge with the right leg in the direction of the point of impact limits the reach.*

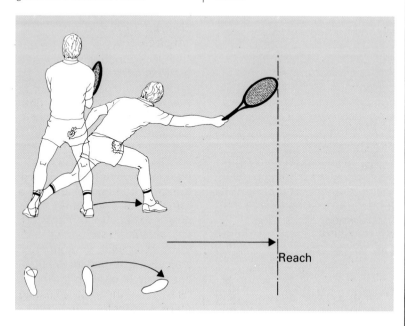

In the case of a ball played gently from your opponent's centre court, and sharply across, you bridge the greater distance from the hitting position by means of a turning step, followed by some normal and natural fast running steps.

ANGLED OR STRAIGHT FORWARD TAKE-OFF AND RUN

Return of service
If time allows (with a slow service), step forward with the leg nearer the point of impact, at a greater or lesser angle depending on the direction of the oncoming ball.

Baseline strokes
You need to run forward from the baseline to reach a ball played by an opponent into the forecourt, or a drop shot. Depending on the location of your starting position and your opponent's placement of the ball, the distance you will need to cover will vary, as will your forward direction.

At the same time as taking your penultimate step, turn your upper body backwards, to a greater or lesser extent depending on the distance of the point of impact and the intended type of stroke, to assist in your backswing action.

In strokes on the forehand side this penultimate step should be taken with your right leg, and in strokes on the backhand side with your left leg.

When making backhand strokes, turn your upper body a particularly long way back, assisting this pivot by taking your left leg past and behind your right leg in the direction of the shot. Before this step your right leg will have braked the speed of your body; as a result of the backward shift your sideways-on hitting position is stabilized, and you will be able to move your weight in the stroke in the direction of the shot.

In both the forehand and backhand strokes, you can take a further changing step to bring you to the ideal distance from the point of impact.

Service line and net strokes

The take-off forward can also be from the service line, as too can the step forwards out of a net position when a ball is to be hit as close as possible to the net: as a half volley or volley, for example.

Snap take-off forward in the direction of the net.

ANGLED OR STRAIGHT BACKWARD TAKE-OFF AND RUN

Return of service

If your opponent's service is coming at you relatively fast and direct you must take a step backwards and to the side, with your right leg in the forehand return, and with your left leg in the backhand return. This gets your body out of the way, and brings you into a sideways-on hitting position.

Baseline strokes

In baseline play you have to move backwards out of the way if your opponent plays very fast and long, aims straight at your body, plays a lob or topspin shot just in front of the baseline, or a smash shot.

The take-off in each case takes the form of a turning step backwards, which is succeeded by follow-up steps, cross-over steps, sidesteps or normal running steps, depending on the direction and distance of the hitting position.

The aim is always to get your body in the hitting position at an angle behind the subsequent point of impact. This applies in a sideways-on or open hitting position and enables you to hit the ball in the most effective way for the particular stroke you are employing.

Service line and net strokes

If your opponent plays a lob shot over you or a very gentle shot past you when you are at the service line or net so that you can no longer get to the ball with a jump, you are forced to run back.

If you want to smash the ball you should take off with a turning step backwards on the right leg (for a backhand smash take-off is with the left leg), and then move with cross-over steps forwards or backwards, with your shoulder line approximately in the direction of the shot, adjusting steps or sidesteps under the subsequent point of impact with the ball.

In some cases you may also have to run back to the net with normal running steps.

Footwork at the moment of impact

STATIONARY HITTING POSITION

Return, baseline, service line and net strokes

A stationary hitting position is when your are standing with both feet on the ground on meeting the ball. This can apply in both a sideways-on and an open hitting position. The more easily you stand in the hitting position, the more reliably you will be able to deliver your stroke. The movement of your weight should always be forwards and in the direction of the hitting action of the arm (upwards or downwards).

When the right leg is brought forward, the front of the feet point in the direction of the shot.

The main advantage of a sideways-on position is that you can continue the follow-through to the optimum length after meeting the ball. You take the last step before the hit in the forehand stroke with your left leg and in the backhand stroke with your right leg. This step should be forwards at an angle in the direction of the point of impact. You rise onto your toes, which point more or less in the direction of the net, to give maximum force behind the stroke.

The size of your steps and the sideways distance between your feet depend on the distance of your penultimate step from the hitting position (or from the

The distance between the feet is a little over hips' width where the point of impact is above hip height.

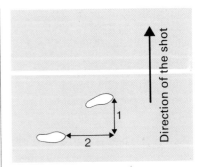

The feet may be close together or more than hips' width apart (1), and paces can be relatively long or short (2).

point of impact). Where the distance is short, your step will be small, and where the distance is greater your step will need to be correspondingly longer to get you into the hitting position. The fine correction for the ideal distance from the point of impact is often made with an adjustment step.

The height of the point of impact, too, influences the distance between your feet. The higher the point of impact,

There must be a considerable distance between the feet for a low point of impact.

Sliding into the hitting position enables the body's momentum to be checked.

An open hitting position in a stroke in which the player has been forced out of the court to the side.

HITTING THE BALL ON THE MOVE

Hitting in motion applies primarily when a step is taken during the hitting action, and so only one foot is on the ground when the racket meets the ball.

Service
In the service, at the point of impact your left foot is on the ground and your right foot in the air; after the racket has met the ball your right foot lands and takes the weight of your body.

Return of service, baseline, service line and net strokes
Very often you hit a stroke on the move when your legs were well apart before playing the stroke. This is particularly so in the return of service and in volley play with the point of impact above net height, but also in positions at the service line and baseline with fast oncoming balls, or if the ball is to be given high speed with the assistance of weight transfer. Even if you have to move backwards out of the way before the stroke this form of footwork may be used for the shot.

You only put your foot – the left foot in the forehand and the right foot in the backhand – onto the ground in the direction of the net when the ball has already been hit. This assists the momentum of the

the closer your feet to each other, the lower the point of impact (as in a low volley or half volley), the further apart they should be.

With your feet wide apart and your knees well bent, your centre of gravity is low, making you very steady, and the stroke properly controlled.

On shale courts, it often happens that a player slides into the final hitting position with the last step. Where possible, this sliding should not be overdone, as it makes it virtually impossible to transfer your weight.

Players slide in particular when the momentum of their body's movement has to be decelerated after fast running over considerable distances, as when running to meet a drop shot from an opponent, or to balls that have to be met on the side, outside the court. Here, the entire sole of the foot is put onto the ground. The stroke can to some extent be controlled because of the

relatively easy position (sideways-on or open).

An open hitting position should be adopted if you are under pressure of time with very fast balls from an opponent (particularly in the forehand or backhand return); if you have been forced to the side way out of court (on the forehand side, rarely on the backhand side) or if you used a stroke such as topspin forehand, for which an open position is better than the sideways-on hitting position.

In an open hitting position it is less easy to transfer your weight forwards. It tends instead to shift more from the ground upwards, which benefits the topspin by giving the required forward spin, or from outside inwards, which will enable you to cover the court again after the stroke.

The player meets the ball while the left leg is still in the air: this applies, for example, in the volley.

stroke through the transfer of your weight.

A variation of hitting in motion consists of the stroke being played not from a walking step, but on the run. This may be necessary, for example, when you are forced to hit the ball from a fast running speed along the baseline, usually also outside the sideline too, which happens most frequently with a passing shot.

In attacking shots too – when you are running towards the net – the ball is often hit on the run. It makes no difference whether the take-off is from the baseline, to return a ball played short by an opponent with an attacking shot (usually the slice), or whether it is from the service line, to hit a relatively slow ball from your opponent over net height as a volley. When playing a stroke on the run

your front foot is still in the air during the hitting action, only reaching the ground after the ball has been hit.

A useful step when hitting the ball on the run is the so-called tango step, which is used in the sliced backhand played as an attacking shot. Here, on meeting the ball, the weight of your body is still on your right leg; your left leg is still in the air at the point of impact, and crosses behind your right leg in the direction of the shot to maintain your sideways-on body position and to take your weight.

There are also some players who, in an attacking shot, jump off from the right leg after meeting the ball, and land again on the right leg.

The spring forwards happens in both the forehand and backhand, from the right leg onto the right leg. Here, at the point of impact and shortly afterwards, your body position is to some extent stabilized, allowing you to meet the ball reliably. In situations in which the ball has to be hit in a backward action for reasons of time, you should try to stabilize your body's position by springing slightly backwards (in the backhand from left to left, in the forehand from right to right).

HITTING THE BALL IN THE AIR

When you hit the ball in a jump, both your legs are in the air at the moment when the

racket meets the ball. You jump up so as to be able to hit the ball at a good point of impact (in terms of height and distance), or with particular force, or even to simply get to the ball.

Service
In the service you jump off to the left; the weight of your body can then be taken on either your left or right leg, depending on the type of stroke and individual delivery of the stroke.

Return of service and baseline strokes
In the return of service you jump off from the leg nearer to the point of contact, to be able to get to your opponent's service at all.

The same applies to situations at the baseline, particularly where the ball has been played wide out to the side by your opponent, and in spite of a fast sprint, you can only get to the ball by jumping. In the case of a topspin shot the push-off from the ground can be so forceful and so early that both your legs are in the air at the time of meeting the ball.

In a topspin forehand or backhand, the jump-off is from your right leg, and for both strokes, you may land on either your left or right leg, depending on the situation and individual action.

Service line and net strokes
At the service line and at the net you often need to jump to hit volleys or smashes. For a

forehand volley you jump from your right onto your left leg, and in the backhand volley, the reverse. In ideal conditions the jump is at an angle forwards, but depending on circumstances you may also have to jump to the side, or even at an angle backwards.

In a smash you jump to the right, your left leg moves backwards and your right one moves upwards and forwards in a counter-balancing scissor action. Your left leg then takes the weight of your body on landing.

In the backhand smash you jump from your left leg, and usually land back on it. Only if the movement of your body was fairly violent before jump-off do you jump from your left leg onto the right one.

The player plays the shot on the run in order to get to the ball.

Returning to starting positions

You should try to return to a good starting position for the next shot immediately after playing a stroke. This starting position is in each case half-way between the angle limits of any possible good return shots by your opponent. You should, where possible, move with your body facing the net. This prevents you from being wrong-footed.

Service
When serving to attack you should run far enough forward to be able to spring into the starting position at the moment when your opponent hits the ball, so that you can take off in any direction. In the service you should usually move to 0.5 to 1 metre (18 inches to a yard) behind the service line.

If not attacking, take a further step, a stopping step, after landing, to brake your body's momentum. Push down with your leg after taking the stopping step, and move into a good court position behind the baseline.

Return of service
Depending on whether you want to run to the net with the return, or to remain at the baseline, you should take normal running steps or sidesteps and cross-over steps, to the best starting position for the next stroke.

Baseline strokes
In the baseline area you should take up a starting position about a metre (yard) behind the baseline. If you plan to hit your opponent's ball well behind the baseline you shouldn't remain in this position waiting for the next ball but must run forwards to the baseline immediately after delivering the shot.

The same applies when you either can't or don't want to run further towards the net after playing a stroke between 1 and 3 metres (yards) in front of the baseline; you must run back to the baseline after the stroke.

The take-off for regaining a good starting position (to cover the court) depends on your footwork during the hitting action and your body's momentum on taking up the hitting position.

There is no problem when hitting in motion or on the run if you want to run further forward. In this case the transition between your footwork before and after a stroke is smooth. It becomes more of a problem when you need to go either to the side or backwards.

In an easy hitting position you can push down from your front leg when hitting from a sideways-on position, or from the outside leg when hitting from an open position.

If you reach the hitting position at a high-speed run you can't do this. You will have to make a further step in the original direction of movement while your racket is following through in a stopping step to stop your body's momentum. The pushdown and therefore the take-off to the side or rear is made from this leg, after the stopping step, by bending your knee to a greater or lesser extent depending on your body's momentum. The stopping step is used in all strokes in which your hitting position is attained with a considerable momentum of your body.

Service line and net strokes
From these positions, do not run back to the baseline. Following an attacking shot you should volley or smash, immediately run in the direction of the net, and should there take up a favourable starting position according to the circumstances. The take-off in this net position is generally via a turning step. It is crucial that your legs should never come to rest during a rally (except in the hitting position); they must be in motion at all times to be constantly ready to move and take off for the spring into the starting position for the next stroke.